australia city living

john gollings

george michell

australia

city living

with 390 color illustrations

pages 2–3 and 208 Emili Fox's converted substation residence in Sydney's Paddington

pages 6–7 Sydney Harbour with the Opera House

pages 8–9 Australian Centre for Contemporary Art, Melbourne, by Wood Marsh

page 9 top to bottom Gallery in the Melbourne Museum by Denton Corker Marshall; Bennelong restaurant in the Sydney Opera House refitted by Dale Jones-Evans; Western Australian Maritime Museum, Fremantle, Perth, by Cox, Howlett, Barley and Woodland, with installation by Cunningham Martyn Design; Woodland bar and coffee shop in Republic Tower, Melbourne, by Fender Katsalidis

page 10 top to bottom Video show in the Australian Centre for Contemporary Art, Melbourne, by Wood Marsh, with light exhibit by Ian DeGrunchy; the Sidney Myer Music Bowl, Melbourne, refurbished by Gregory Burgess Architects; the National Museum of Australia, Canberra, by Ashton Raggatt McDougal; the Melbourne Museum by Denton Corker Marshall; the National Museum of Australia, Canberra; the Melbourne Museum

pages 10–11 Arbour on Brisbane's South Bank by Denton Corker Marshall

pages 12–13 left to right Brisbane's South Bank with arbour by Denton Corker Marshall; Western Australian Maritime Museum, Fremantle, by Cox, Howlett, Barley and Woodland; interior of Power House Centre for the Live Arts by Peter Roy in collaboration with Brisbane City Council Architectural Design; Ondine restaurant in Republic Tower, Melbourne, by Fender Katsalidis; Sidney Myer Music Bowl, Melbourne, refurbished by Gregory Burgess Architects

pages 14–15 Federation Square, Melbourne, by Lab architecture studio in association with Bates Smart

First published in hardcover in the United States of America in 2004 by Thames & Hudson Inc., 500 Fifth Avenue, New York, New York 10110

thamesandhudsonusa.com

Library of Congress Catalog Card Number 2003108924
ISBN 0-500-51146-2

Printed and bound in China by Toppan

contents

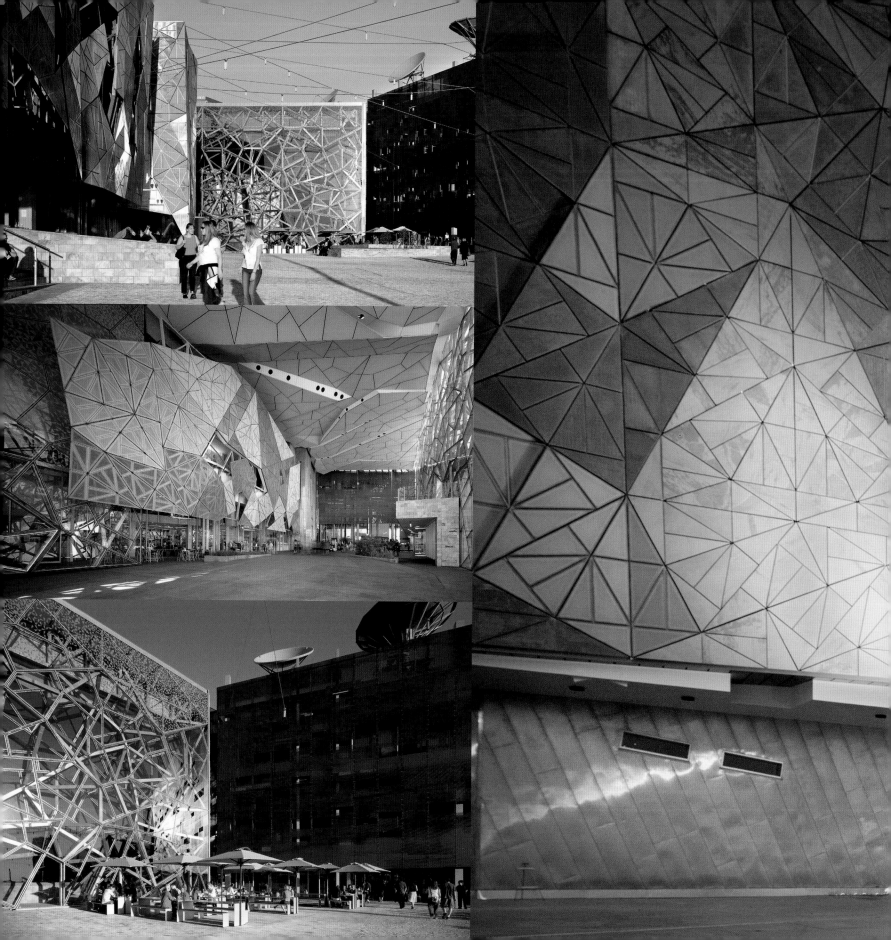

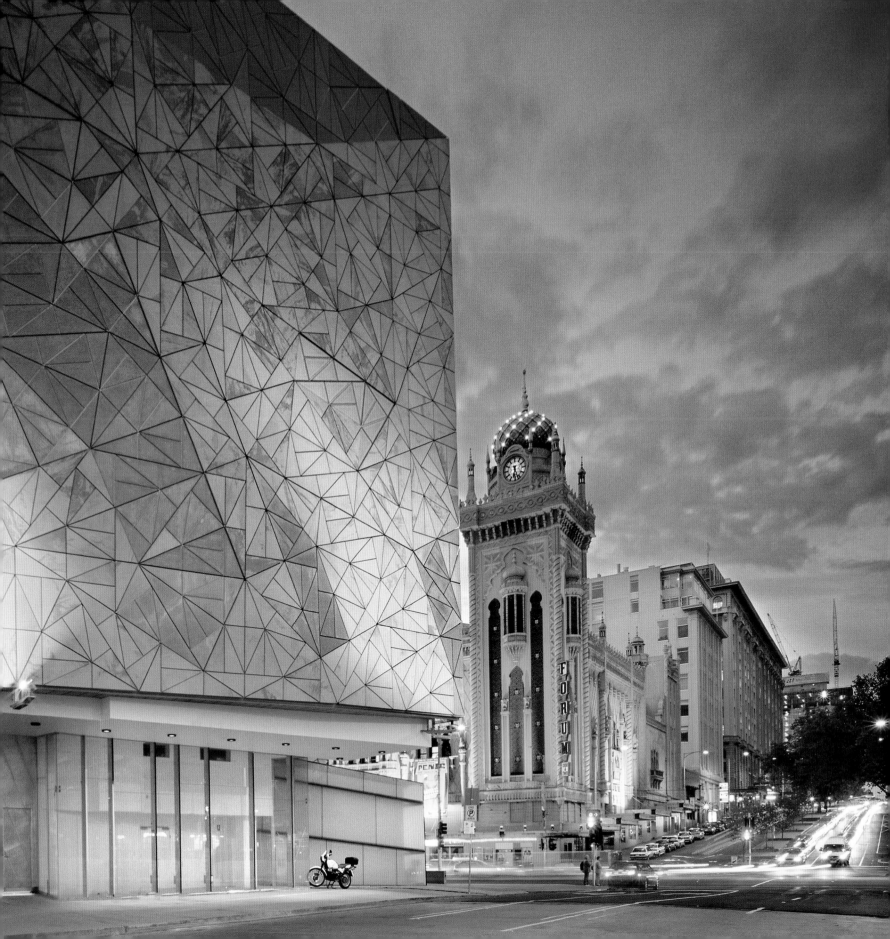

introduction

The rebirth of Australia's inner cities has been under way for some years, but it is only now that the results can truly be appreciated. While Australians have not forsaken their love of beaches and wilderness, nor indeed of sports of all kinds, they have come to eagerly embrace the newly discovered delights of urban life: galleries and concert halls, bookshops and design studios, bars and clubs. Above all, they take enormous pleasure in good food, wine and coffee, as is obvious from the ever growing numbers of restaurants, bars and cafés that line inner city streets. Australians love to spend time strolling, shopping, eating, drinking or simply people-watching, whether beside the water at Circular Quay or Darling Harbour in Sydney, or along Melbourne's characteristic 'strips', such as Chapel Street or Brunswick Street. The recent rehabilitation of these and other similarly popular locales is a testament to the positive economic, social and cultural changes that Australian cities have been undergoing.

Urban Australians feel comfortably cosmopolitan in the post-millennium era. Though they have travelled widely, they now truly value the attractions and advantages of home. Turning their backs on the outer suburbs where most of them grew up, Australians are repopulating the city centres and surrounding areas. The result is an increasing densification of inner urban zones, and a proliferation of purpose-built apartments, townhouses and villas. That the inner cities should have proved a stimulating environment for both architects and their clients may be judged from the spirit of adventure that infuses so many of the projects featured in this book.

The perception of inner cities as desirable places to live is hardly new. Sydney and Melbourne were already vibrant, rapidly expanding metropolises by the end of the nineteenth century. Only after the middle of the twentieth century was there a general exodus to the suburbs. Many of today's inner city residences inherit something of the urban past. They are built on the narrow sites of nineteenth-century residential buildings; they even inhabit disused warehouses and factories. The presence of the past by no means hampers contemporary practitioners. To the contrary, architects like Jackson Clements Burrows in their block of four apartments in downtown Melbourne appear only too willing to reconcile the present with the past. This imaginative exercise in contemporary forms and materials, perched daringly on top of a 1930s building, inhabits the inner city just as naturally as its older support.

above Inner city locations across Australia

opposite Apartments by Jackson Clements Burrows crowning Charter House, Bank Place, Melbourne

inner city lives

Who then lives in Australia's inner cities, and how do they conduct their lives? Central urban locations offer an unrivalled range of possibilities for both employment and recreation. Little wonder that they are irresistible to young people, whether singles or couples, straight or gay. These young urban residents follow flexible work routines at nearby offices; they may even work part- or full-time from home. But young people are not the only ones to appreciate the advantages of inner city living. Older singles or couples, including professionals who remain active participants in urban life, constitute another category of inner city residents. Their children may have grown up and moved out, but this is not always the case. Many of the projects featured in this book have been designed for parents with young children at school, or grown-up children at university or in their first job who still live at home. Other projects accommodate multi-generational families, such as those with an older couple living with their children and grandchildren.

Despite this considerable variation in the composition of urban households in Australia today, there is nonetheless considerable overall consistency in patterns of daily life. To begin with, there is the tendency for city dwellers each to follow an independent routine. Couples and family members rarely get up or go to bed at the same time, and only eat together on special occasions. Even so, the different householders do share a common living space, as is evident from the core area that serves as the hub of most of the apartments, townhouses, warehouse conversions and villas illustrated here. This living space is essentially an empty shell waiting to be filled with activities such as entertaining, reading, watching TV, listening to music and so on. Flexibility of design is essential, since members of the household use this space in different ways and at different times. Other than wall shelves and perhaps a fireplace, living spaces generally rely on furniture and art works to give them individual shape and character. In multi-level residences, the common living space is often fully or partly double height, emphasizing its role as the primary focus of inner city domestic life. Wherever possible, architects add an outlook onto a balcony or court that serves as an outdoor extension of the living area, always an attractive option in Australia's warmer climates.

Most inner city living spaces have designated eating zones, though only in larger dwellings are formal and family dining distinguished. In contrast, cooking areas are conceived as subsidiary spaces, thanks to the compact, high-tech stainless steel stoves, sinks and fridges that are so popular today. The

typical urban kitchen is reduced to a freestanding bench for food preparation, often with sink on top and storage beneath, and an adjacent wall-mounted stove with vent. The fridge and other amenities, including laundry, are usually tucked well out of sight behind cupboard doors. Such minimal kitchens are invariably located within or next to the main living or dining space, so as not to segregate cooking activities from everyday family life; gone are the days when housewife or host disappeared into the kitchen to prepare a meal.

If inner city households have little or no separation between living and dining zones, the same is certainly not true for bedrooms, which are conceived as discrete spaces for the children and parents or even individual partners to retreat from one another. This is true even when the bedrooms are located on a mezzanine, with visual and aural communication with the living-dining area below. Most dwellings have more than one bedroom, though in the smallest apartments and townhouses a second sleeping zone can sometimes only be created by means of sliding or folding doors. Inner city residents demand bathrooms that open off their bedrooms, with wardrobes in between. They prefer showering to bathing, which explains the profusion of separate glassed-in cubicles. They also insist that the wet areas of the bathroom be

distinguished by the use of ceramic, stone and glass.

In spite of their proximity to inner city amenities, Australian urban citizens are still dependent on cars. Open space is obviously at a premium in city locations, so wherever possible parking is incorporated within the fabric of the house, generally as a garage beneath the living area. Lack of open space also means lack of gardens, and residents often have to be content with walled-in, planted courts. No doubt this is one of the reasons so many urban dwellers aspire to a second home at the beaches or in the forested wildernesses that lie only an hour or two from most Australian cities. The ideal, it seems, is a double life conducted in both an inner city and an out-of-city residence.

from left to right Living area of penthouse in Sentinel Apartments, Surfers Paradise, by Willemsen Development Corporation; Kitchen-dining zone in Stephen Jolson's factory renovation, St Kilda; Kitchen in the warehouse conversion of Wood Marsh in Prahran; Outdoor seating in the rooftop apartment designed by Nick Bochsler in South Yarra; Children's bedroom in the Toorak villa of De Campo Architects; Bedroom in Gary Marinko's villa, Dalkeith; Bathroom in the penthouse of Bill Krotiris of Fender Katsalidis in HM@S, Port Melbourne; Garage adjoining Chris Clarke's villa in Taringa

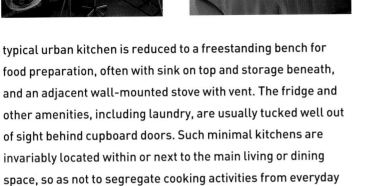

inner city styles

If the living habits of urban families in Australia conform to definable patterns, then it makes sense to expect the same of the architectural styles of their inner city residences. What is apparent is that a contemporary approach to architectural design has finally found widespread acceptance in Australia. There is now an abundance of newly completed, modernist dwellings, not to mention an explosion of lifestyle shops selling sleek furniture, much of it influenced by the latest French and Italian models. Contemporary design has firmly established itself as the accepted visual expression of Australia's cosmopolitan urban culture.

While, as always, only a handful of architectural projects meet the highest aesthetic standards, there is now a considerable amount of activity, attracting many of the most talented practitioners. This is mainly due to an ever-widening circle of clients with sufficient wealth at their disposal and a growing confidence in contemporary design. Both individual clients and property developers have commissioned leading architects to design many of the high-density residential complexes springing up all over Australia's inner cities. The result is a profusion of fine quality, contemporary styled projects crowding the waterfront around Sydney's inner harbour and the previously abandoned docklands and riverfronts of Melbourne and Brisbane. Here and in other inner city locations, apartments and townhouses combine with shops, restaurants, galleries and cinemas to achieve a quintessential urban mix of facilities and functions.

As it turns out, the contemporary idiom that characterizes the brilliantly creative projects featured here – whether apartments, townhouses, warehouse conversions or urban villas – is composed of a trio of closely related styles. These are defined more by virtue of the materials, textures and colours they deploy than by any particular formal or spatial qualities. Modernist rigour is far and away the most popular of the three Australian inner city styles. This is probably because its clean lines, whitewashed surfaces, glass expanses and occasional metallic accents are perfectly suited to the glare of the Australian outdoors, as well as the limited natural light available to some inner city residences. Though modernism may appear at first to be an essentially simple style, it demands considerable skill in the handling of proportions and details. Among the finest masters are the Sydney architects Engelen Moore, as is evident from the strict geometry and seamless textures of their diminutive townhouse in Surry Hills. Judging from their luminous, all-white apartments in Republic2, East Sydney, the designers Burley Katon Halliday are also

experienced modernists. However, few architects can match Ed Lippmann's modernist rigour, as expressed in his villa in Sydney's Vaucluse.

Visual splendour and tactile comfort are the keynotes of urban opulence, another distinct trend in Australian inner city styles. Here there is a preference for rich warm tones, such as brown-grey, beige and chocolate, and luxurious textures, such as deep soft carpets and suede coverings, or dark wooden veneers and painted lacquered surfaces. All these features come together in Alexander Michael's apartment at the end of the refurbished Woolloomooloo Finger Wharf in Sydney. The extravagant interiors are animated by lime green and pale pink walls as well as specially commissioned metallic sculptures and Italianate paintings. Andrew Parr achieves a more sombre, though no less sumptuous effect in his penthouse in HM@S, Port Melbourne, by combining polished granite floors and white marble fittings with dark coloured walls and fabrics.

For some architects and their clients, the rigours of modernism hold few attractions and the excesses of urban opulence remain unattainable and perhaps undesirable. Instead, there is always industrial chic, the newest of these modernist styles to gain acceptance. This has its origins in the architecture of warehouses and factories; hence the emphasis on steel-framed construction, polished concrete surfaces and glass louvres. Turning its back on comfort and softness, industrial chic aims at a more brutal elegance. This is evident even in domestic details, such as the stainless steel kitchen bench in Chris Clarke's villa in Taringa, Brisbane. A similar hard-edged stylishness is seen in the metallic sheets and brightly painted panels that clad Shelly Penn's warehouse conversion in Melbourne's Richmond.

But whether it is the abrupt collisions of industrial chic, the comforts of urban opulence or the rigours of modernism, inner city architecture in Australia today is consistently charged with an irrepressible aesthetic inventiveness.

from left to right Engelen Moore's townhouse in Surry Hills; Sitting area in Wood Marsh's warehouse conversion in Prahran; Living area and bedroom in one of the apartments in Republic2, East Sydney, by Burley Katon Halliday (two photographs); Upper Gallery of Ed Lippmann's villa in Vaucluse; Balcony of Shelley Penn's warehouse conversion in Richmond; Kitchen in Chris Clarke's villa in Taringa; Formal seating in the waterside apartment by Alexander Michael at the end of Woolloomooloo Finger Wharf

apartments

apartments

A dusk panorama of the city skyline from one of the penthouses on top of Engelen Moore's Altair apartment block in Sydney's Kings Cross provides the perfect backdrop to sophisticated inner city living. Elevated above the street and accessed through a well-guarded lobby, a high-rise residence such as this offers urban families a centrally located refuge in which they can willingly embrace the spectacle of the city as they go about their everyday routines. This desire to overlook the urban panorama so as to incorporate it into the family living space has now become something approaching an obsession. Architects respond by creating high-rise apartments with generous expanses of glazing that open onto spacious terraces and balconies.

Nowhere is the attachment to urban views better demonstrated than in Harry Seidler's Horizon Apartments in Sydney's Kings Cross. Confidently ignoring the more humble scale of the surrounding streets, this forty-three-storey tower presents a vertical stack of continuous, interweaving curved balconies that survey the city from all sides. A less lyrical, but no less balconied elevation is that of Sentinel, one of a cluster of residential blocks that overlook the river at Surfers Paradise, Queensland, now Australia's fastest growing urban centre. However, few apartment blocks can equal the heroic exterior of Republic Tower in Melbourne's city district. The prow-like balustrades that cantilever dramatically over the street are trademarks of the architects Fender Katsalidis, to be repeated in their HM@S Beach Apartments in Port Melbourne, where the nautical protrusions are echoed in the ocean-going ships that dock at the pier below. Even in less conventional schemes, such the renovated silo project in Hobart's

Harry Seidler's Horizon Apartments in Kings Cross, Sydney

Salamanca Place by the architects Heffernan Button Voss, the apartments are articulated by projecting balconies.

The architects Tonkin Zulaikha Greer offer an alternative approach to the treatment of balconies by partly coating the heavy masonry exterior of their apartment block in Potts Point, Sydney, with lustrous, richly toned copper tiles. In his Macquarie Apartments in downtown Sydney, Renzo Piano opts for a seductive transparency, sheathing fourteen storeys of balconies in a continuous façade of adjustable glass louvres. These glassed-in terraces offer incomparable panoramas of the Royal Botanic Gardens and harbour beyond. But for total transparency, no project can match the Marquise apartments in Melbourne's St Kilda by Urban Design Architects. This curvilinear building has nineteen floors of apartments encased entirely in glass: the only protection from the glare is from the strips of aluminium louvres that continue around the open prow-like balconies at the tips of the building. Architect Nick Bochsler devised a quite different solution to creating transparency and lightness in his rooftop apartment in South Yarra, Melbourne, by transforming the balcony into a pool of reflective water. Only a portion of the terrace is used as an outdoor sitting area; the remainder is filled with water falling sheer out of sight.

Aside from framing spectacular city views and enhancing the exterior aspects of high-rise buildings, balconies wrapping around one or more sides of an apartment also fulfil the more practical function of extending the interior space to provide alternative outdoor living and dining areas. By entirely glassing in the balcony, Renzo Piano has created an intermediate zone

Sentinel apartments in Surfers Paradise, Queensland, by Willemsen Development Corporation

Hobart's Salamanca Place silo apartments by Heffernan Button Voss

between inside and outside. Another original approach is that taken by Burley Katon Halliday in the duplex residence of their Republic2 complex. Two outdoor zones flank the living area here: one an inward-looking private court; the other an outward-looking balcony surveying the shared swimming pool and lotus pond below. Where a second level is available, as in the penthouse above one of the high-rise blocks in Allan Jack + Cottier's multi-unit Moore Park Gardens development in Sydney's Redfern, there is the opportunity for a rooftop terrace, with swimming pool and glassed-in sitting area. In contrast, the duplex residence of Republic2 features a more private deck opening off the bedroom.

Architects must also consider carefully the interior layouts of high-rise apartments, many of which demand tight planning. Almost all have a core living-dining area, into which a kitchen is incorporated at one end or to the side. While kitchens are typically reduced to a minimum, this does not preclude the introduction of eye-catching gleaming surfaces. In his penthouse in Republic Tower, Nonda Katsalidis places the white marble kitchen bench in front of a wall-mounted stove with a stainless steel vent flanked by similarly metallic storage cupboards. An inventive alternative are the service pods that efficiently compress the kitchen, laundry and bathroom into a single freestanding unit in the apartments in Rushcutters Bay, Sydney, designed by the architects Engelen Moore. The pods are visually emphasized by the use of distinctive bright colours that stand out against the otherwise whitewashed walls of the living and sleeping quarters. By contrast, Burley Katon Halliday hide the kitchen zone altogether behind a storage unit at the end of the core living space. In a more expansive scheme like the penthouse of Allan Jack + Cottier, the dining-kitchen area is at a slightly different level from the core living zone.

Urban Design Architects' Marquise apartments in St Kilda

Living areas in high-rise apartments are generally conceived as single open spaces, sometimes furnished in the lavish manner characteristic of urban opulence, though practitioners such as Engelen Moore promote a more rigorous modernist approach, as can be seen in their Altair project in Kings Cross. Clients commissioning larger apartments and penthouses sometimes require formally discrete living spaces. In the waterside residence at the end of the refurbished Woolloomooloo Finger Wharf in Sydney, for example, the designer Alexander Michael has created a sequence of zones intended for meetings and grand entertainments rather than everyday living. The same seems to be true of the grandly scaled, double-height spaces of the Katsalidis penthouse in Republic Tower. Here, there is a continuous movement between formal and informal sitting and dining areas. In Andrew Parr's penthouse in the HM@S Beach Apartments, the double-height living area is clearly set apart from the single-height dining-kitchen area.

Wherever possible, living and sleeping zones in high-rise buildings are separated, but only in larger residences can the bedrooms and bathrooms be in a dedicated wing. More usually, space is at a premium and apartments have to accommodate living and sleeping zones within the same overall space. In their Potts Point apartment, Tonkin Zulaikha Greer have chosen a mezzanine solution, with the bedroom looking down on the double-height living area. A gallery runs from the bedroom and over the living space to protrude somewhat theatrically over the end balcony. In his coolly elegant, single-level rooftop dwelling, Nick Bochsler reduces the main bedroom to an annex with a sliding door so that it may be closed off from the main living space. Even so, a separate guest bedroom and bathroom are also provided.

surrounded by water

above The whitewashed apartment on top of an older commercial building with railway tracks below

left Furniture in L-shaped formation defines the living zone

Light floods into this apartment built on top of an older commercial building in Melbourne's South Yarra. Architect Nick Bochsler has created a lofty living-dining area with a 4-metre-high (13-foot) ceiling lit by windows on two sides. A terrace beyond extends the living space, at least visually; outdoor seating is only possible between spreading palm trees at the end because the terrace is otherwise given over to a shallow pool that reflects and refreshes, the water falling sheer out of view. A sliding door in one corner of the living area gives access to the master bedroom; the kitchen is located in another corner.

surrounded by water

left Plastic stools beneath a white marble bench in the kitchen, with windows surrounding dark wooden cupboards

below The bedroom opening off the living area

above The terrace pool runs alongside the dining-living area

high-density utopia

Moore Park Gardens in Sydney's Redfern feels like a utopian experiment in high-density living, accommodating up to one thousand people. Two apartment blocks as well as rows of multi-level townhouses, some with private courts at ground level, others with rooftop balconies, face an internal planted walkway shaded by trees and pergolas. There is also a private street for parking, as well as a shopping centre, café and swimming pool. As if to temper the grandiose scale of the development, the architects Allan Jack + Cottier employ a diversity of materials and textures: different coloured bricks, painted stucco panels, glass balustrades, and steel overhangs, awnings and balustrades.

opposite above Grosvenor Apartments, one of two high-rise blocks that tower over the townhouses in Moore Park Gardens

opposite below The planted walkway linking the apartment blocks to the townhouses

above Kitchen with living area beyond in the penthouse in Dowling Tower designed by Tim Allison

high–density utopia

above Master bedroom with pivoting bookcases at either side of the bed

left Living area with steps leading up to the kitchen-dining zone in the penthouse in Dowling Tower

louvred outlook

Designed by the celebrated Italian architect Renzo Piano, the Aurora Place office building and its shorter companion, the apartment block known as Macquarie, have brought architectural distinction to downtown Sydney. All of the fifty-six apartments on fourteen floors in Macquarie have full-width terraces with magnificent views over the Royal Botanic Gardens. The terraces are entirely glassed in, but can be opened up by manipulating banks of louvres. Both living and kitchen zones have sliding glass panels that open onto the terrace; a separate glassed-in breakfast area actually projects onto the terrace. Side walls covered with Italian terracotta tiles add a warm flourish to the otherwise fully glazed interior.

opposite left The complex from the street

opposite right Sculpture by Kan Yasuda in Aurora Place

top The Sydney cityscape framing Aurora Place

above The lime green lobby of Macquarie

louvred outlook

opposite above left Louvres in the open position

opposite above right The façade of Macquarie, showing the electronically adjusted louvres in closed, half open and fully open positions

opposite below Outdoor dining on the glass louvred terrace in one of the apartments in Macquarie

above Kitchen and breakfast area in one of the apartments in Macquarie, seen from the adjoining terrace

sumptuous atmosphere

Located on the fourteenth floor of an undistinguished building on Melbourne's St Kilda Road (originally built for the Defence Department), this apartment designed by Michael Bialek and Andrew Parr of SJB Interiors benefits from high ceilings and uninterrupted panoramic views on three sides. The interior is conceived as a series of interconnecting spaces, appropriate for the lifestyle of a professional couple who entertain frequently. A sumptuous atmosphere is achieved through the use of dark colours and fabrics, timber floors and elegant wooden furniture and fittings.

above Living area framed by a view of the city

opposite above Dining area with stained wooden table, painting by Ross More and an original Mackintosh chair; the kitchen beyond has stainless steel suspended shelves

opposite below left The gleaming surfaces of the bathroom opening off the master bedroom

opposite below right Living area by night

quayside classical

East Circular Quay complex by PTW Architects blends
a classically inspired colonnade and entrance rotunda
with contemporary materials and design to achieve a
quintessentially urban idiom appropriate to Sydney's
harbour setting. The complex consists of three adjoining
high-rise buildings incorporating two apartment blocks and
Mirvac's Quay Grand hotel, designed in collaboration with
HPA Architects, together with a number of restaurants,
bars, cafés and cinemas.

opposite Glass-roofed walkway leading to the promenade beside
Sydney Cove, with Sydney Harbour bridge in the background

above The trio of high-rise buildings that form East Circular Quay;
the curving glass balconies belong to one of the apartment blocks

right The rotunda with a patterned granite floor and mobile
sculpture by the artist Peter Cole

quayside classical

left and below The colonnade at promenade level lined with shops and cafés

left The staircase ascending from the promenade gives access to one of the restaurants of the complex

below Living area in one of the residential suites in Mirvac's Quay Grand, with view of Sydney Harbour bridge

quayside classical

right Bathroom in a residential suite of Mirvac's Quay Grand

opposite Swimming pool in Mirvac's Quay Grand

below Sitting area in one of the suites overlooking the Royal Botanic Gardens to the rear of the complex

uncompromising simplicity

Rising over a traffic tunnel in Sydney's Kings Cross, the Altair apartment building designed by Engelen Moore presents a simple yet rigorous grid of glass panels and concrete balconies. A similar uncompromising simplicity infuses the interiors, nowhere better seen than in the grey silvery tones and elegant Italian furniture of one of the penthouses that occupies the top level. Here, polished concrete, stainless steel and lacquered woodwork are animated by light coming in from full-height windows on two sides. Balconies beyond offer incomparable views of the city and harbour. A spacious L-shaped living-dining area serves as the core of the penthouse; bedrooms and bathrooms are accommodated in a separate wing.

left The Altair block rising over a multi-level car park and car showroom

below The L-shaped living-dining area in one of the penthouses

above The white marble-like resin bench in the kitchen faces onto the sitting area and balcony

below left Skylit bathroom opening off the master bedroom

below right The penthouse's master bedroom

over the street

In this apartment block in Potts Point, Sydney, the architects Tonkin Zulaikha Greer have ingeniously combined six residences with different single- and double-level layouts. On the street the block presents deep balconies framed by a sinuous panel of lustrous copper tiles that creates an asymmetrical cubist-like composition. The apartment shown here maximizes the available double-height space by placing the bedroom and bathroom at mezzanine level. From here a gallery runs somewhat melodramatically across the space and out over the rear balcony.

above The mezzanine gallery running from the bedroom and passing through the end glass wall

right The apartment block has deep balconies that project over a popular restaurant and bakery at street level

opposite left The mezzanine gallery dominates the double-height living-dining area of this apartment

opposite right Wooden steps leading to the bedroom with the steel-mesh floor of the mezzanine gallery running to one side

total transparency

The Marquise is a jewel-like, double-curved building with pointed tips at two ends rising above Melbourne's St Kilda. Urban Design Architects have sheathed the nineteen storeys of apartments entirely in glass, thereby achieving an effect of total transparency. Aluminium-framed louvres run continuously around the building, protecting the interiors from glare and heat, while giving views on all sides. The interiors by Carr Design Group employ unpainted concrete and grey and beige tones to complement the metallic structure. Natural wood is used sparingly for the floor of the kitchen area and the fitted cupboards in the TV den and bedrooms.

opposite above left The Marquise at night

opposite above right The reflecting pool extending outwards from the lobby

top Balcony at the prow-shaped end of the building

above left and opposite below The interiors are defined by their curved outer walls of glass

whitewashed luminosity

Occupying a whole block in East Sydney, the Republic2 development consists of an extended L-shaped wing of apartments entered from one corner along a diagonal corridor. Lotus ponds and a swimming pool raised on a terrace in the middle of the development serve as a visual and social focus. The bold whitewashed masonry forms, metallic louvres and glass balustrades are hallmarks of Burley Katon Halliday, the designers responsible for the project. The apartments include this duplex residence, which has a private internal court as well as an external balcony looking out over the swimming pool and the city skyline beyond.

left Living area with external balcony beyond

opposite above Louvres and deep balconies characterize the street façades

opposite below View of the city from one of the duplex residences

below Private internal court with turquoise fish tank filled with crystal

whitewashed luminosity

below Outdoor dining on the external balcony

right The curtained living area with private internal court beyond

bayside grandeur

opposite Living area looking out over the bay

left Double-height glazing of the penthouse facing onto the terrace

below left Kitchen with pale grey lacquered cupboards and white marble panels

below Steps leading up to the balcony and master bedroom beyond

The ambitious residential development known as HM@S takes its name from the former HMAS naval yard that once occupied this site in Port Melbourne. Twin towers with characteristic prow-like tips rise above five-storey podiums that include this penthouse designed by Bill Krotiris of Fender Katsalidis architects. Its interior is dominated by a grand double-height living-dining area. Glazing opens onto a terrace with an uninterrupted vista of Port Phillip Bay. The side wall is punctuated by masonry panels and voids that conceal the home office below and master bedroom at mezzanine level above.

opposite above This penthouse in HM@S, designed by Andrew Parr, has a double-height living area

opposite below The dining area with its two-tone polished granite floor and dark coloured walls and furniture; the painting is by Imants Tillers

top The living area, with Italian marble light stands

above left Master bedroom

above right Dark-toned bathroom opening off the master bedroom

disciplined minimalism

left Balcony view from one of the apartments looking towards the Victorian row houses opposite

below The kitchen-dining space flowing seamlessly into the living area beyond

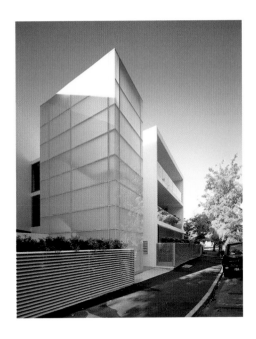

The architects Engelen Moore have incorporated twenty-six apartments of seven different layouts into this double residential block in Sydney's Rushcutters Bay. The deeply shaded balconies of the apartments complement those of the nineteenth-century row houses on the other side of the street. However, the white and grey concrete, aluminium louvres and clear and translucent glass combine to create a crisp geometry that is entirely contemporary. The typical interior consists of a single living-dining space with a full wall of cupboards for storage and amenities on one side, and sliding glass panels opening onto a balcony on the other: a perfect setting for disciplined minimalist living.

top left Staircase block with translucent glass walls

above left Louvred corridor linking the apartments

top right The apartments are in two blocks, one angled to the street

above right Looking out from the bedroom of one of the apartments

luxury on the water

With extravagant interiors designed by Alexander Michael for a leading Sydney businessman, this vast apartment at the end of the redeveloped Woolloomooloo Finger Wharf is intended for formal meetings and grand entertainments rather than everyday living. The apartment occupies the whole of one floor, with decks overlooking the water on three sides. The interior consists of separate sitting and dining areas linked by lobbies and offices, with sitting-out areas on the deck. A sense of luxury is sustained throughout by the use of dark walnut veneers, lacquered and glass surfaces, and specially commissioned reproduction Italianate paintings. A substantial kitchen services the apartment but there is only a single bedroom-bathroom suite.

above Outdoor dining on the deck

left Metallic sculptures created by Alexander Michael

below Sitting area with dining room beyond

luxury on the water

above Entrance lobby with modern
Indonesian paintings imitating Italian
Renaissance works

opposite top left The internal kitchen
is intended for large-scale catering

opposite top right Bathroom clad in
translucent glass sheets

opposite below Another sitting area

bold urban statement

Soaring above the streets of downtown Melbourne, the cantilevering prow-like balconies of Republic Tower epitomize the bold urban statements for which the architects Fender Katsalidis are now celebrated. Indeed, this is only the latest in a series of high-rise projects that dot the Central Business District. The uncompromising structural skeleton of this 100-metre-high (330-foot) building is fashioned in untreated concrete, relieved only by stainless steel fittings, clear glass balustrades and dark tinted glazing. Its thirty-six storeys mostly accommodate apartments with single living-dining spaces and three bedrooms opening off narrow terraces. But there are also several luxuriously appointed, multi-level penthouses at the top of the tower, including one designed by Nonda Katsalidis himself. An unusual feature of this project is the changing display of artworks at street level sponsored by the Visible Art Foundation Project set up by Katsalidis' own development company.

right The bold concrete forms of Republic Tower. Corner image by Patricia Piccinini

left Cantilevering prow-like balconies of the upper apartments

below Lap pool at the thirty-third level

bold urban statement

above Limestone-floored common lobby
of Republic Tower; the painting is by
James Clayden

left Corridor inside the penthouse, with original builders' graffiti

below Formal double-height living space, with paintings by Tony Tuckson and Steven Harvey

bold urban statement

above Formal double-height dining space

opposite above Corridor linking the formal living-dining space with the kitchen-family room, with an artwork by John Davis on the wall; the stairs ascend to the bedrooms

opposite below Bedroom with ensuite bathroom

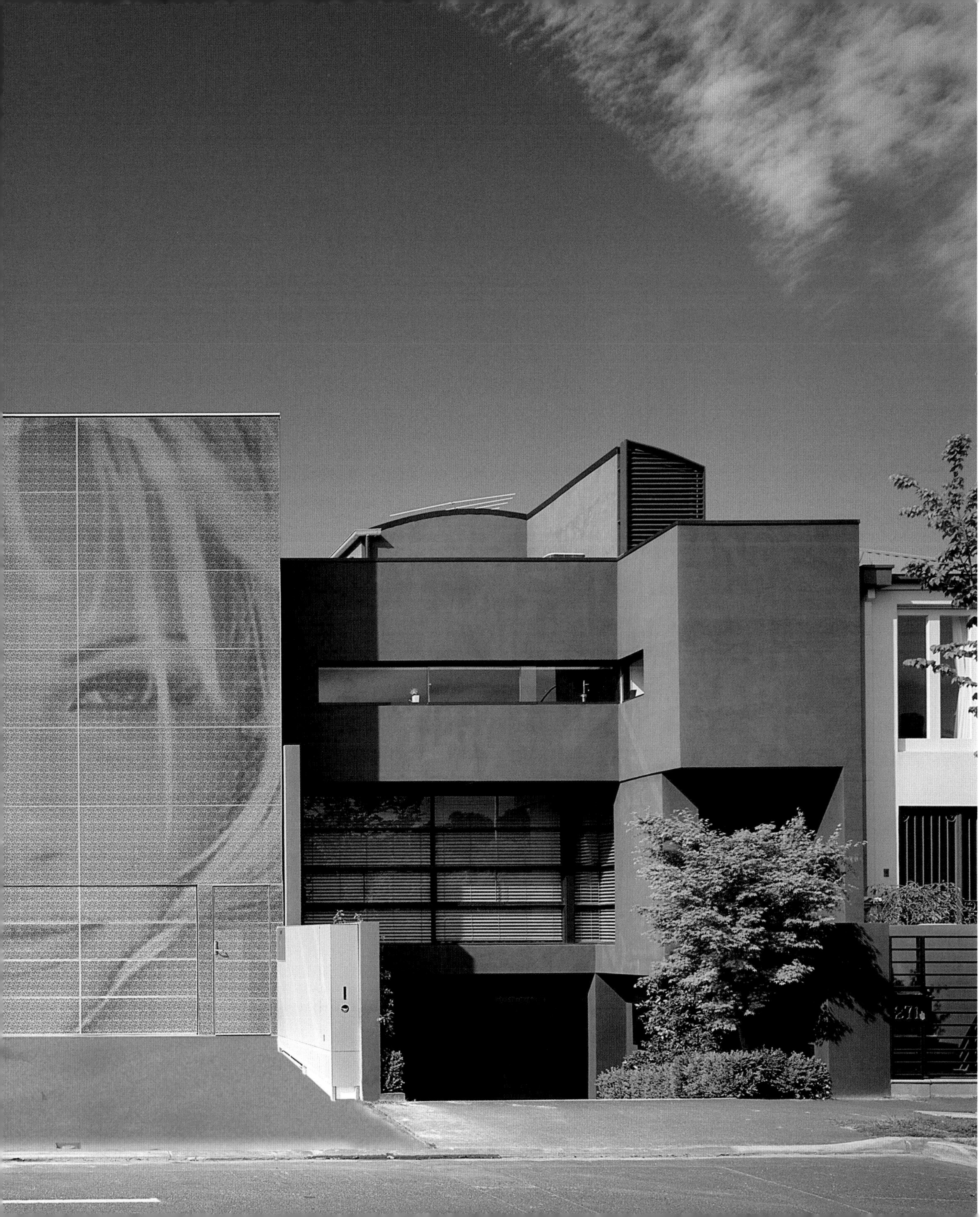

townhouses

townhouses

A photograph of Pamela Anderson borrowed by the architect Cassandra Fahey from a popular TV show and printed onto a façade of blue glass panels punctuates a row of new townhouses in Melbourne's St Kilda. But behind this provocative and highly unconventional façade is an interior layout not so different from that of the many townhouses springing up in Australian cities today.

Townhouses are built on long narrow sites typical of nineteenth-century Australian cities. The cottages and mansions that once occupied these plots have fallen victim to neglect or unenlightened planning and subsequent demolition. Like the structures they replace, new townhouses occupy the full widths of the sites, touching the boundary walls on either side. In order to exploit the available space in between, architects create a single living area without any side corridor. Since a spatial distinction between eating and living is no longer considered necessary, the kitchen-dining zone is generally incorporated into this living area. This poses few problems since cooking activities tend to concentrate on a single freestanding bench and a food preparation area recessed into the wall. But that is not to suggest that such minimal kitchens lack individual character: witness, for example, the brilliant red and black bench and storage cupboards designed for a block of townhouses in Melbourne's Prahran by the architects McBride Charles Ryan.

Most townhouses are multi-level, with bedroom and bathroom above the living area and, wherever possible, parking and other services at street level, as in the trio of almost identical dwellings by Cunningham Martyn Design in Richmond, Melbourne. On rare occasions, parking and living are combined on a single level and even visually linked through a glass wall, as in the St Kilda steel-framed house by Andrew

Kitchen in Dale Jones-Evans' townhouse in Elizabeth Bay

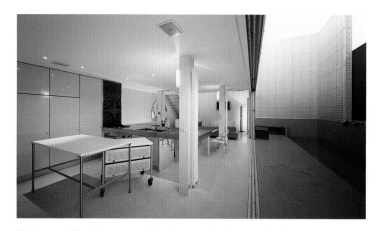
Kitchen with adjacent pool in Cassandra Fahey's St Kilda townhouse

Kitchen in one of McBride Charles Ryan's townhouses in Prahran

Parr of SJB Interiors. Spatial fluidity is sometimes achieved by opening up the living space to make it fully or partly double height, overlooked by one of the bedrooms. In Prahran, McBride Charles Ryan combine five 'downstairs' and five 'upstairs' townhouses in an ingenious interlocking scheme. Living areas are located at both bottom and top levels, while the bedrooms are wedged in between. Another means of gaining space is to expand the bedroom into a private living zone, complete with sitting area, walk-in wardrobe and bathroom. Sam Marshall's rooftop addition to a terrace house in Balmain, Sydney, is conceived as an independent suite, with distinctive colours and lighting. Another rooftop scheme is that of Paul Gillett, who vertically extends the residential space of his central Adelaide house by providing a canopied full-length terrace. This has provision for outdoor living and dining, as well as a fine view of the Adelaide hills in the distance.

Staircases placed against the side walls have the effect of liberating the core living spaces; when situated in the middle they serve to separate the living and kitchen-dining zones; on occasion, they even become a major architectural feature. In the townhouse in Elizabeth Bay, Sydney, designed by Dale Jones-Evans, the steps are encased in glass and lit by a skylight; there is even a reflective pool at the bottom. Cassandra Fahey, in the St Kilda 'Pamela' project, places illuminated orange plastic panels beneath open-mesh metal steps to introduce a brightly coloured accent to an otherwise monochrome interior.

Lighting the interior is always a problem in a long narrow house. Most dwellings face directly onto the street, which means that the house cannot be opened up at the front without compromising the family's privacy. The architects Lahz Nimmo use wooden slats to screen the front windows of their

Jackson Clements Burrows' townhouse in Richmond

townhouse in Newtown, Sydney, and also repeat the device at the back where it is not required for reasons of privacy. In their project in Richmond, Melbourne, the architects Jackson Clements Burrows employ translucent and coloured glass to create a vivid street elevation that also ensures privacy. More common are townhouses with deep windowed balconies at the upper level that provide both privacy and light, such as the example by the architects O'Connor + Houle in Melbourne's South Yarra. However, not all townhouses conform to this arrangement. Peter Tonkin of Tonkin Zulaikha Greer and Ellen Woolley cloak the street elevation of their narrow residence in Sydney's Lilyfield with a brick wall broken only by slit windows, which insulates the interior against traffic noise.

Architects are generally much less restricted in their treatment of the rear of townhouses, which they often glaze so that light can flood in from floor to ceiling. The project of Stanic Harding in Surry Hills employs sliding glass panels and pivoting louvres on three levels to achieve total transparency. Another strategy to bring light into the interior is to create a glassed-in court. Allan Powell's South Yarra townhouse focuses on a densely planted internal garden overlooked by the living area and kitchen at ground level, and bedroom and den above. Skylights, too, are common to almost all of the projects featured here. But few interiors are lit with as much skill and imagination as that of Nicholas Gioia's living-dining extension to a nineteenth-century cottage in South Melbourne. As well as a circular skylight, this has a cross-shaped side window and unusually canopied rear windows.

The long, narrow sites on which most townhouses are built invariably result in long backyards. These are settings

Townhouse in Lilyfield by Peter Tonkin and Ellen Woolley

for outdoor living and dining, with table and chairs, food preparation bench and often a barbecue. Backyards are usually paved with concrete, tiles or pebbles. Planting is generally restricted to hardy bushes, bamboos and trees, perhaps with an ornamental pond fed by a small waterfall. Where backyards are sufficiently long, an independent structure may be erected at the end to serve as an office, den or gym, thereby transforming the yard into an internal court with blank side walls. In the townhouse of the architects Marsh Cashman in Sydney's Woollahra, a glazed office den is set at the end of a pebbled court shaded by an exotic Brazilian tree, with a lap pool on one side. At the end of the backyard in Dale Jones-Evans' house is a small pond with a gym above. The gym is concealed from view by a seemingly floating metallic mesh that ensures privacy from the neighbours, while at the same time serving as a visual focus for the court. Where townhouses are set back-to-back, as in the project by Six Degrees Architects in Fitzroy, Melbourne, backyards may be combined to create common courts separated only by a low fence. However, in such cases, slit windows and skylights are essential to preserve privacy between dwellings.

Such a diversity of solutions testifies to the imagination and ingenuity of a host of present-day architects of townhouses. Nowhere is this better seen than in the remarkably thin, metal-framed residence in Brisbane's Fortitude Valley designed by Codd Stenders. This showpiece of virtuoso lightweight steel technology achieves maximum circulation and space in an exceptionally narrow house. Additional space is even 'borrowed' from the street below by metallic sun louvres that angle outward.

above Codd Stenders' townhouse in Fortitude Valley

right Rooftop living in Paul Gillett's townhouse in Adelaide

strict geometric grid

This two-storey steel-framed townhouse in St Kilda, Melbourne, designed by Andrew Parr of SJB Interiors, is regulated by a strict geometric grid of 3.5-metre (11½-foot) squares. The metallic construction and white walls and ceiling are relieved by the dark colours and warm textures of the carpets and furniture. The kitchen-dining-living area at ground level runs between an open court at the front reserved for car parking and a narrow walled garden at the rear. There are two bedrooms above, one with a private sitting space that overlooks the living area below.

left The house from the street with a garage on the left and a double-height open court for additional parking on the right

opposite A small landscaped garden at the rear of the house brings light into the living area, from where steps ascend to the bedrooms and bathroom

below The dining area is dominated by slabs of sumptuous streaked black marble which encase the kitchen bench and cooking area

inspired extension

This inspired brick extension to a Victorian period house in South Melbourne was designed by Nicholas Gioia for a couple when they had a new child. The new wing is divided into a double-height dining-kitchen zone and a single-height living area with steps ascending to a private den for the parents above. Scrupulously detailed both inside and out, the new wing has ingeniously placed wall recesses and fittings and unusually shaped windows, some with overhangs to counteract the morning glare. The external brickwork is glazed so as to contrast with the fabric of the original house.

above View of the new wing showing the cross-shaped window on the side and the larger areas of glazing shielded by bold overhangs at the back

right Kitchen-dining area inside the new wing

above A bright red ceiling marks the division between the original house and the new wing

below Steps to the private den at the upper level

above As well as the cross-shaped window in the side wall, the new wing is lit by a circular skylight

elegant compression

above The stone mosaic rear wall of the pebbled court with a small pond in front

left The three levels of the house open up to the court

left Built-in storage lining the staircase

below The dining area is in the middle of the house

Completely refurbished by the architects Stanic Harding, this townhouse in Surry Hills, Sydney, is a study in elegant compression, as expressed in the resourceful economy of the layout and the fine craftsmanship of the built-in furniture and fittings. Natural timber floors, lacquered woodwork and translucent glass panels generate a calm atmosphere, while the walls of sliding glass at each level of the house ensure an abundance of light. The entrance from the street opens onto the kitchen, with the dining-living area beyond leading to a small balcony. Steps against the side wall descend to a sitting-guest room beneath, with access to the outdoor court. There is a bedroom suite situated above.

green priorities

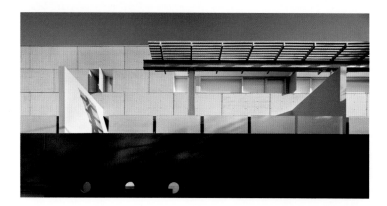

top and centre The three townhouses seen from the street

above A louvred overhang shades the balcony that opens off the living-dining area

This trio of almost identical townhouses occupies a compact corner site in Melbourne's Richmond. As conceived by Cunningham Martyn Design, the dwellings exploit passive solar heating and natural cooling so as to be energy efficient and to minimize environmental impact. The exteriors are partly clad in thermal cement sheets, while the interiors use low toxicity plywoods. The dwellings are arranged on three levels, with small pebbled court, garage and children's bedroom at ground level; living-dining area with corner kitchen zone opening onto a small balcony at the intermediate level; and master bedroom with ensuite bathroom at top.

above, below and opposite right Living-dining area at the intermediate level, with corner kitchen; the rear wall is lined with hoop pine plywood cupboards, with skylight above; the open stairway ascends to the bedroom

behind the icon

Cassandra Fahey's house for a well-known sports personality in Melbourne cheekily punctuates a street in St Kilda by presenting a screen-like façade entirely covered with an image of actress Pamela Anderson. Entry is almost invisible since the front door and garage are concealed in the green-blue panels that cloak the façade. Though made of glass, the panels are opaque, which means that there is no visual communication between the interior and the street. Another unusual feature of the house is that the main living-dining space, and the small court and narrow lap pool it opens onto, are situated on the first upper level, above the garage. From there, steps ascend to the master bedroom.

above With its glass-clad street façade printed with a photograph of Pamela Anderson, the house contrasts strikingly with the continental modernist dwellings to either side

left The glass wall of the kitchen-dining-living area slides open onto the side court and lap pool

below The living-dining space at the first upper level overlooked by the master bedroom balcony

behind the icon

left The house seen from the pool, with corrugated translucent fibreglass sheeting and glazing wrapping around the upper levels

below Master bedroom with a wall of clear and opaque glass panels

below right Stairway with steps of perforated steel lined with orange plastic sheets that are illuminated from below

solutions in steel

This multi-storey house was designed by Codd Stenders for an academic and his wife on a long narrow piece of land less than 3.5 metres (11½ feet) wide in Brisbane's Fortitude Valley. Flexibility of design within such spatial constraints is achieved by means of a virtuoso steel structure reinforced by diagonal braces built up against a retaining side wall. On its street façades, the house is clad in painted steel panels alternating with glazing shielded by outward angled metallic louvres that ensure privacy. The principal level of the house consists of a walk-through kitchen leading to a dining space with a living zone beyond, separated by a central staircase. A gallery looking down onto the dining space at the first upper level links the two bedrooms. Tucked into the angled roof are a study and den.

opposite left The steel-frame construction with outward angled louvres dominates the street; the entrance to the double garage is at ground level

opposite right The central staircase is set free from the retaining side wall

above The house is built on a narrow corner site between a newly widened road and the retaining side wall of a commercial property

left Gallery linking the two bedrooms on the first upper level

solutions in steel

left Walk-through kitchen just inside the street entrance; the painting is by Ronnie Tjampitjinpa

top The living zone beyond the central staircase is screened from the street by angled metallic louvres

above Master bedroom on the first upper level

screened and slatted

above Rear of the new wing showing the angled roof and slatted screens of the study at the upper level; the slatted screen below is angled outwards to serve as a canopy

left Japanese-style rear garden at night

Designed for a professional who works partly at home, this house extension in Newtown, Sydney, pits the new against the old. The architects Lahz Nimmo have added a two-storey wing to one side of the Victorian property, with wooden slatted sun screens and a bold angled roof that make no concession to the original street façade. The rear of the house is more coherent, for here the architects have remodelled the original building so as to harmonize with the slatted screens and metallic balcony elements.

below The renovated living room in the original house, with newly created windows opening onto the garden

below The dining-kitchen extension with wooden floor and veneered cupboards, looking towards a small garden court at the front

above Study at the upper level with angled roof and skylight running the full length

below Steps from the kitchen-dining extension to the upper level

raising the roof

Sam Marshall's rooftop bedroom suite built onto a Victorian corner house in Sydney's Balmain is animated by colour and light. The bright red and yellow of two of the walls are echoed in the red bed coverings and reddish timber floor. Windows are cunningly positioned to frame a view of the city, or to admit light without sacrificing privacy. Wall recesses for storage maximize the usable space of the bedroom, while creating a cubist-like play of shapes and planes.

above House from the street showing the rooftop addition

above right Kitchen at ground level in the original house

opposite above Inside the bedroom suite at the top of the house

opposite below, left to right Painted wooden slats cover the side wall next to the steps that ascend to the bedroom; Corner bathroom clad in red tile mosaic; Window seating with city view at the end of the bedroom; Wall recesses in the corner of the bedroom

industrial domestic

Occupying a tight corner site in Melbourne's South Yarra, this townhouse by O'Connor + Houle Architecture makes innovative use of industrial materials in a domestic context. Bare polished concrete frames the deeply cut openings of the master bedroom and balcony on the upper level at the front of the house; the same material is used in the floor of the living-dining area beneath, while also extending into the small walled-in court in front. In contrast, the side façade of the house is clad in translucent corrugated plastic sheets, with sliding panels for access to the garage below and slit windows for the children's bedrooms above. The translucent plastic sheets glow at night.

opposite above left The concrete front façade with deeply cut window openings and balcony

opposite above right Side façade of pale green corrugated plastic, illuminated from within

above left Steps with imaginative metallic banisters

opposite below Theatrically cantilevered kitchen bench with living area beyond

above right Green glass table in the dining area with painting by Howard Arkley

below Living and kitchen areas, with the cantilevered bench

warmly toned elegance

opposite above Living area with light streaming in from the garden court

opposite centre left Master bedroom with slit windows in the rear wall

opposite centre right White marble and timber veneers in the bathroom beyond the master bedroom

above The plain stuccoed street façade, with bougainvillaea climbing over the garage

below The kitchen-dining area with a wall of wooden storage cupboards, and the garden court beyond

Allan Powell's tightly planned townhouse in Melbourne's South Yarra exploits solid stucco surfaces and natural hardwood finishes to achieve a warmly toned elegance. Turning its back to the street, the house focuses on a small but densely planted interior court that brings light into the living-dining area and kitchen, as well as the bedroom and study den at the upper level. Additional natural light is introduced by shallow slits in the rear wall of the living area and master bedroom above.

right Marble sink in the walk-through bathroom between the entrance and garage

far right A glass wall screens the living area from steps ascending to the bedrooms

interlocking living

left The crumpled concrete façade cut by horizontal slit windows runs over the garages

opposite above left Dining area of one of the 'downstairs' houses opening onto a private garden court

opposite above right Internal bathroom

below The block from the street

This multiple residential block in Melbourne's Prahran incorporates ten townhouses with two different layouts devised by the architects McBride Charles Ryan. Their interlocking arrangement provides private garden courts at the back of five 'downstairs' houses, and open decks at the top level for five 'upstairs' houses. All of the bedrooms and bathrooms are located on the intermediate level. Textural interest on the exterior is created by a combination of crumpled concrete, curving zincalum and timber slats. Then there is the contrast between the vertical surfaces and the gentle curves of the roof. The interiors benefit from sloping walls and curved ceilings, as well as occasional splashes of bright colour.

above Kitchen bench with red-painted wall of cupboards containing the cooker

interlocking living

left Internal bathroom of one of the 'upstairs' houses

opposite The pool framed by a curving timber slatted wall at the front of the block

below Bedroom with low windows and curved ceiling

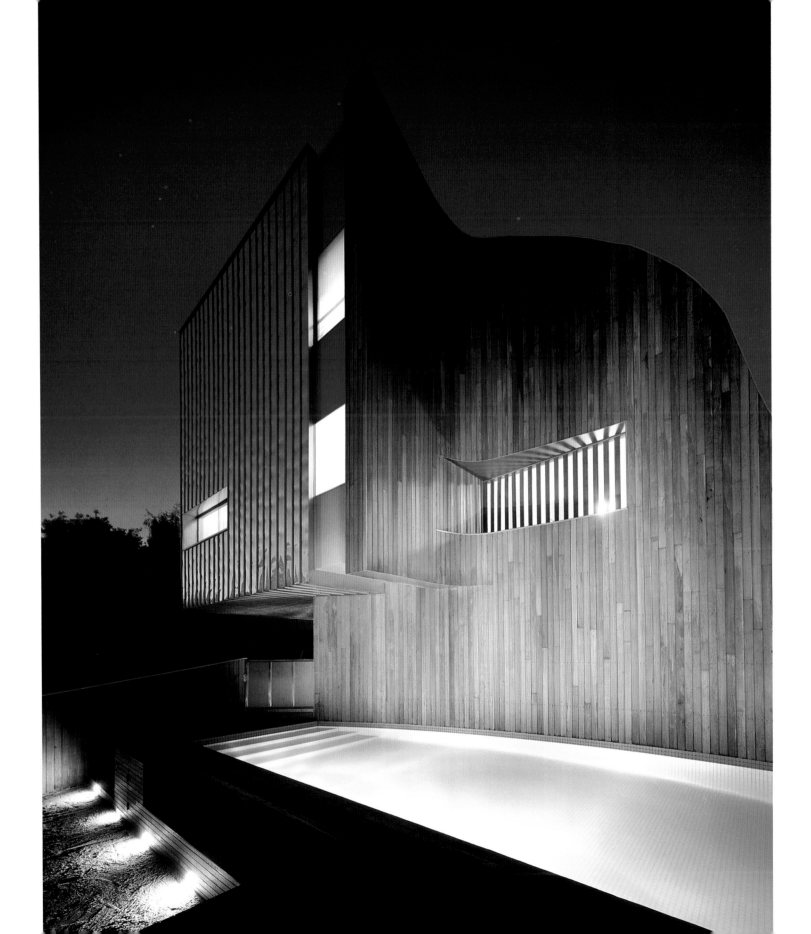

back-to-back planning

One of a set of four townhouses set in back-to-back pairs within the structural framework of an old factory, this project in Melbourne's Fitzroy illustrates the virtues of ingenious and economical planning. The houses are all laid out in the same fashion, with the garage and storage at street level, living-dining-kitchen area on the first upper level linked to a den or spare room opening onto a small court, and bedrooms and bathroom at top. Throughout, Six Degrees Architects have provided built-in dining table and bookshelves, thereby gaining space for the narrow living-dining area that runs from the front of the house to a small court at the rear. The wooden floors and whitewashed walls and ceiling contrast with the bright yellow and mustard colours of the built-in fittings.

opposite above left Coloured glass in the windows of the living area

opposite above right Small court at the rear of the living area looking onto the back of an identical house facing the opposite direction

opposite below left The living-dining area on the first upper level with steps leading up to the bedrooms and bathroom

opposite below right The end of the living-dining-kitchen area

right The double façade of the twin townhouses, with garage below and living area above

angled surprises

Tucked away at the back of Oxford Street in Paddington, Sydney, this intriguing development comprises residential extensions to the upper floors of two shops and a separate townhouse above a parking lot at the rear. The architect Angelo Candalepas was intent on preserving the existing trees that dot the site so he devised a complex angular scheme around them using fibro panels, wooden louvres and projecting windows. These disparate elements are unified by abruptly oblique forms and dense coloured patterns. Even the garden court, with its seemingly random arrangement of brick paving, old timbers and stone blocks, is angular and surprising.

opposite above Residential extensions at the rear of the two shops with living areas above and sheltered sit-outs below

opposite below left The townhouse seen through the trees of the garden court

opposite below right The townhouse from the alley to the rear of the site, showing its wall of louvred windows

above left Angled corners of the living area in the townhouse

above Kitchen opening onto the living area

bringing light in

In his inspired reworking of a nineteenth-century townhouse in Sydney's Elizabeth Bay, Dale Jones-Evans is mainly concerned with bringing light into the interior. The central stairwell that articulates the interior has a generous skylight that admits light into the middle of the house, illuminating the living room at the bottom level and the bathroom and library-TV den at the intermediate level. Meanwhile, outdoor light is filtered by the filigree mesh screen that floats over the front door of the house as well as the gym at the end of the rear court. All these features are hidden from the street by the Victorian period façade that remains unchanged.

above left The original townhouse from the street

above right A filigree metallic mesh screens the front door

right The three storeys as seen from the rear court

opposite Stainless steel bench and seating area in the kitchen

bringing light in

opposite above left Master bedroom in the restored gable roof

opposite above right Staircase well illuminated from a skylight above

opposite below Library-TV den at the first upper level

above left Bathroom with ceramic fittings and glass walls

above right and far left Filigree metallic mesh screening the gym at the end of the rear court

left Steps leading up to the gym

cool and contemplative

In this townhouse in Woollahra, Sydney, the architects Marsh Cashman have used polished concrete and whitewashed surfaces accented by zinc and stainless steel sheets to create a contemplative atmosphere for a professional couple interested in literature and art. Such cool materials contrast with the warm colours of dark wooden floor-to-ceiling shelves that run around the outer walls of the study at the front of the house. Filled with books, the shelves serve as a focus for the double-height living area in the middle. A kitchen-dining zone at the rear of the house opens onto a long court with a narrow lap pool on one side and a small office den at the end.

above The kitchen with polished concrete bench and stainless steel cooking area opening onto the rear court

left The house overlooking the rear court with lap pool

cool and contemplative

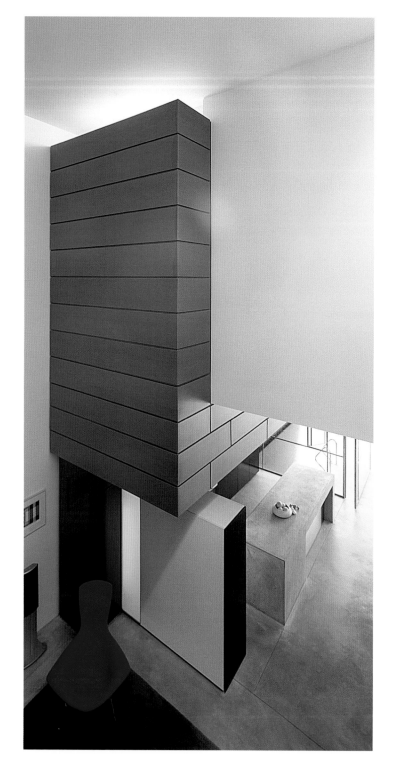

above Living zone overlooked by the gallery

opposite left The zinc-encased bathroom 'box' above the kitchen

opposite right The living zone with small study at one end,
bookshelves wrapping around its walls

industrially textured

right The house is clad in corrugated steel interrupted by bands of translucent polycarbonate sheeting and occasional wooden louvres

below left Bedroom gallery

below right Bedroom gallery with bathroom at the end

This diminutive three-storey townhouse in West Melbourne is clad in industrial derived materials that give it a richly textured appearance that harmonizes with the surrounding factories and warehouses. The architects Jackson Clements Burrows have used corrugated steel and translucent polycarbonate sheeting in combination with wooden and glass louvres to achieve both light and privacy. Somewhat unusually, the principal living-dining-kitchen zone is at mid level, with a bedroom gallery in the steeply angled roof above, and a second bedroom and bathroom below opening onto a small court.

below Living-dining area lit by louvred windows

above left Entrance to the house from a side lane

above right The bathroom at ground level opens onto a small court

conversions

Bird de la Coeur's factory conversion in Albert Park with office below and residence above

conversions

The curving wall of glass that rings the circular court in the middle of Kerstin Thompson's warehouse conversion in Melbourne's Fitzroy testifies to the imagination of an architect working under considerable constraint: converting an inner city warehouse into a spacious family home. Not merely content with transforming a factory into a comfortable and serviceable residence, Thompson sought to create a visually exciting experience. The resulting project is one of many innovative solutions to the challenge of accommodating present-day urban dwellers within the fabric of older industrial buildings.

In times past the inner zones of Australian cities were crowded with factories, workshops and warehouses; but as manufacturing declined in the late twentieth century, many of these buildings came to be neglected and abandoned. At the same time there was a growing appreciation of these disused but centrally located industrial structures as desirable places to live and work, especially among urban professionals, who eagerly relocated their residences here, sometimes also their offices and studios. Such factories and warehouses also came to serve as public venues, especially as theatres and art galleries, restaurants and cafés. These rehabilitated residential, professional and recreational projects represent a striking confrontation of old and new, adding industrial-archaeological dimensions to inner city living.

Because of extensive building restrictions in the inner zones of Australian cities, architects are often compelled to leave untouched the outer fabric of an industrial structure and can make little or no alteration to the street elevation. So it is sometimes impossible to tell that behind a derelict brick façade with rusting factory doors and windows there is a sparkling new residence. In Sydney's Paddington, for example, the architect Emili Fox has retained the gabled façade and entrance of a small electrical substation, but inside has built a triple-storey townhouse with its own internal court. In some instances architects have left the interiors of warehouses in their original condition, complete with untreated peeling brick walls and worn timber trusses. Such is the case in Shelley Penn's diminutive studio-residence within a former grain storage warehouse in Melbourne's Richmond.

Offices and studios are often combined with residences in warehouse conversions. The architects Jones Coulter Young have taken an old tannery in Fremantle outside Perth and within its unrestored external walls have erected a suite of four offices with parking. At the rear stands a newly built, two-storey townhouse with its own planted walkway and pool. Also common are multi-level combinations of work and living spaces, with office or studio at street level and residence above. In their factory project in Albert Park, Melbourne, the architects Bird de la Coeur thoroughly renewed the interior of the building while preserving the original sliding door and window openings.

In addition to their unrivalled locations in the heart of the city, industrial buildings offer another prime advantage: space. Many of these factories and warehouses enclose substantial volumes spanned by wooden trusses or steel beams carrying corrugated iron roofs with skylights. They offer architects unique opportunities for creating free-flowing roomy environments on more than one level. There is, however, a constant problem of lighting and ventilating the interior, since warehouses are generally built up to the edges of sites with little or no surrounding open space. While architects are only too willing to replace or enlarge factory windows and skylights, clients sometimes feel the need for an additional

Kitchen in Kerstin Thompson's Fitzroy project

source of light and air. In response, architects may strip away part of the roof cladding to create a zone that is open to the sky. In the Albert Park project of Bird de la Coeur, a roofless terrace at the upper level is converted into a planted garden with children's play area and outdoor dining.

A more elaborate roofless space forms the core of Graham Jahn's residence in Surry Hills, Sydney. In this project, the original industrial interior has been opened up to create a court with lotus pond, overlooked from one side by a newly built, triple-storey townhouse; there is even a small meditation chamber at the end. This same architect's predilection for courtyard living is illustrated in another of his warehouse projects, this one in Sydney's Redfern. Here, the principal living-dining zone wraps around a double-height court into which the kitchen bench extends for outdoor eating. Slit windows at the upper level give views from the bedrooms above. A second smaller court introduces light into the guest room beyond. In their rehabilitation of an industrial block in Prahran, Melbourne, the architects Wood Marsh have created a spacious terrace opening off the main living-dining zone. This terrace is punctuated by a swimming pool painted bright red and framed by the original factory walls covered in foliage. Kerstin Thompson's warehouse conversion, already mentioned, introduces a glazed circular court into the middle of the house. This drum-like space supplies light and air to the interior, and also serves as a dramatic visual focus for the everyday activities of family life.

While the internal proportions of warehouse residences are obviously dictated by the existing perimeter walls, architects

Access corridor in the warehouse conversion of Jones Coulter Young in Fremantle exercise considerable inventiveness in maximizing the available internal space. Wood Marsh, for example, opt for a free-flowing living-dining zone that is partly shielded from the entry by angled masonry walls. Evidently the clients felt the need for some refuge from this airy openness for within this zone the architects created an enclosed, womb-like elliptical pod for TV viewing. Most conversions segregate the bedrooms and bathrooms from the main living area. This is sometimes achieved by means of multiple levels, as in the two residences of Graham Jahn or the Fremantle tannery project of Jones Coulter Young. An unusual approach is to vertically stack the different zones of the house on two or three storeys. In their conversion of an old coach house in West Melbourne, Bird de la Coeur opened up the interior to accommodate a flight of steps that ascends from the garage and den at street level, to the bedrooms and bathrooms at the middle, and from there to the living-dining kitchen area at the top of the house.

Stephen Jolson is equally resourceful in his ingenious reworking of a commercial space in Melbourne's St Kilda. Jolson provides definition to the required living areas by creating a service pod standing freely within the perimeter walls. The kitchen-dining zone is partly accommodated in this pod, but also expands into the main living area, while the bedrooms, bathroom and laundry protrude into a corridor-like space behind. The fact that the architect here dispenses entirely with solid partitions and doors only helps to focus attention on the original dimensions of the commercial space and its metamorphosis into a flexible and efficient inner city residence.

Wooden trusses above the living area in Graham Jahn's Surry Hills factory residence

warehouse metamorphosis

This triple-level residence designed for an art collector in Sydney's Surry Hills occupies a 1920s timber yard, with original brick walls and wooden roof trusses left untouched by the architect Graham Jahn. The house is entered from the street by descending to an open court bounded on one side by the newly built residence clad in metal louvres, glazing and wooden screens. A panelled concrete wall provides structural stability to the core of the house, which has the living-dining area at the first upper level. Sleeping accommodation is segregated, with the children's bedrooms at ground level beside the court and the master bedroom at the second upper level.

above View of the house, at the intersection of three lanes, showing the transition from original brickwork to new wood panelling and corrugated metal cladding, with the corner entrance to a double garage

opposite left Skylit lobby, with a door in the panelled concrete wall leading to the children's bedrooms, and steps ascending to the living-dining area; the painting is by Todd Hunter

opposite right Entrance court with lotus pond, timber slatted meditation chamber at the end, and to the side, the new residence with metal louvres shielding the children's bedrooms below and the glazed balcony of the living-dining area above

warehouse metamorphosis

left Living area at the first upper level roofed by 15-metre (50-foot) wooden trusses supporting sky lighting, with a panelled concrete end wall; the painting is by John Hoyland

above Living-dining area with paintings by Paco Perez Valencia and Freddy Tims

below Master bedroom at the second upper level

adventurous rehabilitation

Wood Marsh are the architects responsible for this adventurous rehabilitation of an industrial brick block in Melbourne's Prahran, the top floor of which has been transformed into a spacious family home for a couple with three boys. Retaining the perimeter walls and window openings of the original building, the architects have added freestanding walls and glazing to create a series of interconnecting spaces that showcase a fine art collection. Part of the area is left unroofed to serve as a terrace with a startlingly bright red painted pool. Entry to the living-dining-kitchen area is defined by detached rusticated masonry walls, with a wall of pivoting glass panels opening up to the terrace. An elliptical TV pod encased in concrete is lined with crimson fabric.

above Planted walls of the original building overlook the terrace and pool

right The dining area and TV pod as viewed from the swimming pool

overleaf left Living-dining area with sculpture by Clement Meadmore

overleaf right Crimson materials and cushions line the womb-like TV pod

adventurous rehabilitation

service pod flexibility

Designed for a single young professional, this reworking of a commercial space in St Kilda, Melbourne, was intended to function with maximum flexibility. Accordingly, the architect Stephen Jolson added a service pod to one side of the rectangular space, with kitchen utilities facing a dining zone in front, and two bedrooms, a laundry and bathroom at the rear.

The floor of this pod is raised to accommodate the required plumbing, but otherwise stands freely within the warehouse space, which wraps around it on four sides creating a living area in front and a corridor at the sides and rear. The original warehouse walls and window openings are untouched, permitting light to flood in on three sides.

below The raised floors of the bathroom, laundry and bedrooms, jutting out of the pod

below One of the bedrooms within the pod, partly defined by curtains

above and right above Kitchen facilities are set into the walls of the pod, while the dining area projects away from it

low-cost living-working

The architect Shelley Penn has taken a straightforward approach in creating this low-cost living-working space in the disused grain store of a vinegar factory in Richmond, Melbourne. Leaving the original brickwork and timber trusses intact, she has divided the industrial space into two levels, with a studio beneath and a kitchen-living area above. To this she has added a new bathroom and bedroom block in stainless steel panels, brightly painted walls and louvred windows, thereby achieving striking contrasts of styles and materials. The mobile kitchen bench and living room seating were designed by the client, a graphic designer who also works as an artist.

above View of the factory building from the street

right Kitchen-living area in the roof of the original factory with purpose-built seating and bench

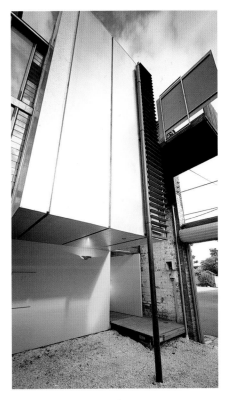

above Side court for car parking overlooked by the metal-clad block containing the bathroom below and bedroom above

left Glass wall of the bedroom as viewed from the balcony

far left Swivelling glass door leading to the small balcony

textures old and new

The conversion of an old tannery in Fremantle, Perth, into an office complex with a residence at the rear served as a pretext for the architects Jones Coulter Young to juxtapose old and new materials. The perimeter walls of the tannery, with unrestored decaying brickwork, were left untouched, providing a frame within which the new structures stand more or less freely. These consist of a number of offices with their own car parking space, as well as the self-contained residence. A narrow corridor conceived as a Japanese garden running along one side of the complex leads to the two-storey home with its own end court and swimming pool.

opposite above Verandah with a canvas canopy that shelters the court and pool below

opposite below The living area at the lower level looks out onto the access corridor and end court

left Bedrooms at the upper level with living area below

The two-storey residence seen from the swimming pool in the end court

The access corridor beside the residence has been designed as a Japanese garden

Decaying brickwork of the original perimeter walls and the lime green coloured walls of the new offices

The walls, sliding door, window and timber joists of the original tannery, with a new fibreglass roof

within substation walls

right The gabled inner wall of the original substation as seen from the court

opposite above Dining area with kitchen set into a wall of white lacquered cupboards

opposite right The living-dining area at ground level, with slatted screens shielding the bedroom windows above

opposite below Master bedroom with skylight at the top of the house

below The street façade of the substation

Built within the perimeter walls of a disused electricity substation in Sydney's Paddington, this house by Emili Fox rises above a newly created internal court with a small fishpond. The ground level is a single living-dining area that runs from the court in front to a cascade of water falling over a tiled wall in a small light well at the rear. Stairs lead to bedrooms on two levels. Those overlooking the court at the front have windows shielded by slatted wooden screens that provide a warm contrast to the surrounding concrete and whitewashed surfaces.

vertical stacking

This imaginative renovation of an old coach house in North Melbourne by Bird de la Coeur Architects retains the street façade and perimeter walls, while entirely remodelling the interior. This is conceived as a set of vertically stacked boxes, partly clad in metal or glass, to accommodate the sleeping and living zones above, linked by a centrally positioned staircase. The ground level serves as a garage for the owners' collection of vintage cars (recalling the original purpose of the building), with a small office and open court at the back. The first upper level is for the bedrooms and bathrooms, while living and dining take place at the top level, from where there are fine

views over the city. Despite tight planning, the spaces flow easily from one level to the next, thanks to the use of reflective and translucent materials, as well as metallic mesh screens.

opposite above Outdoor living at the top of the house with a night-time panorama of the city

opposite below House from the street, showing the entrance to the original coach house

left Garage with the owners' collection of cars, overlooked by the boxed-in bathroom and gallery above

vertical stacking

right Corridor space leading from the street entrance to the staircase in the middle of the house, with slit windows in the side wall giving glimpses of the garage

opposite above Gallery at the first upper level linking the two bedrooms, with guest bathroom in between

below Kitchen-dining area opening off the living room with a glass wall that slides up and over to give access to the balcony

opposite below Living room at the top level, with side wall of glass and fireplace at one end

around the drum court

Once a factory producing sheet metal for filing cabinets, this industrial structure in Melbourne's Fitzroy now serves as a spacious residence for a professional couple and their grown-up children. While retaining the original brick perimeter walls and timber trusses, the architect Kerstin Thompson solved the problem of bringing light into the factory interior by creating a drum-like circular court surrounded by glass panels, around which flow the living, dining and cooking areas. The only enclosed zones are two small studies and the kitchen scullery. A staircase wrapping around the drum ascends to the master bedroom suite at the rear of the house, with additional stairs leading to a rooftop sitting area. A self-contained apartment for the children is located above the street entrance.

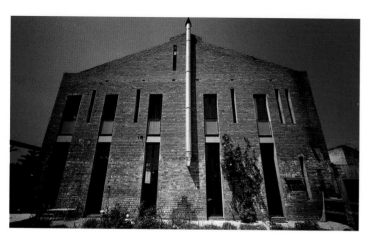

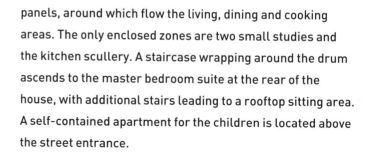

above Covered rooftop sitting area above the master bedroom suite

left Rear façade of the factory with newly created slit windows overlooking a small garden

opposite above left The drum court protruding above the roof as seen from the rooftop balcony over the children's apartment

opposite above right and below The interior spaces flow freely around the glassed-in drum court

around the drum court

above The master bedroom suite at the rear of the house

above right Gleaming ceramic and glass fittings in the bathroom opening off the master bedroom

right Living area beneath the master bedroom suite

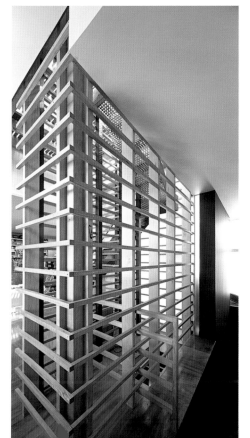

above and left A staircase enclosed by a slatted screen ascends from the entrance to a self-contained apartment for the children, and from there to a rooftop balcony

refigured factory

Graham Jahn has converted a factory on a corner site in Sydney's Redfern into an art gallery at street level and a two-storey residence above. The house focuses on an internal court with a spreading frangipani tree at the first upper level, onto which the living-dining area opens by means of sliding glass panels. The court is bounded by a bright maroon red wall on one side, and a guest bedroom on another; slit windows in zinc-clad walls look down from above. The top level is conceived as a private wing with a master bedroom and sitting area opening onto a small deck at the front.

opposite above The former factory from the street showing the residence rising above the original roof level

opposite below Living-dining space opening onto the court

above The kitchen bench extends into the court as an outdoor dining facility

below The court with its potted frangipani tree

urban villas

urban villas

Opening out into the Perth twilight, Michael Patroni's imposing house in Peppermint Grove epitomizes the ideal of the Australian urban villa as a spacious, though tightly planned luxurious residence. Many such urban villas are now being built on inner city sites, generally in districts that were once suburban with large garden plots, but which are now increasing in density with a corresponding reduction in the size of available land. They are built on land between existing older properties and retain something of the scale and comfort of their neighbours, but are more compact in layout. They also lack the generous tree-shaded lawns and flower beds. Indeed, gardens are hardly possible at all, unless reduced to miniaturized, Japanese-inspired arrangements of rocks, bamboos and ponds, as in the exquisitely crafted planting that surrounds and partly conceals Andrew Nolan's villa extension in Sydney's Paddington. A garden also dominates the layout of Peter Skinner and Elizabeth Watson Brown's villa in St Lucia, Brisbane, where the living area has a wall of sliding glass panels that open immediately onto a gnarled poinsettia tree.

Though the space around urban villas is invariably limited, clients often persuade their architects to incorporate a swimming pool, even if it has to be tucked into one side of the site, as in the house by Andrew Nolan just mentioned. Here, a lap pool runs immediately beside the living-dining kitchen zone, separated from it only by a glass wall that extends beneath the water. Alternatively, the pool may be incorporated into the front terrace of the house, with a low wall to shield it from the street, as in the villa in Melbourne's Toorak designed by Christopher de Campo and Genevieve Nevett. Where more land is available, there is the opportunity to make the pool a major feature, as the architects Donovan Hill have done in

Rooftop planting in Andrew Nolan's villa extension in Paddington

their extension to a traditional Queensland house in New Farm, Brisbane. The pool here is flanked by accessory structures and aligned with the central corridor of the original house. In Patroni's grandiose Perth project cited above, the swimming pool serves as a fulcrum in the L-shaped arrangement of the two residential wings.

Some architects dispense entirely with external outdoor space. Gary Marinko's villa in Perth's Dalkeith occupies most of the site and is entirely inward looking. The rooms face onto two internal courts, one roofed with metallic louvres, the other open to the sky. This unusual scheme achieves a fluid relationship between interior and exterior that is appropriate for the warm, dry Western Australian climate. Queensland, too, offers possibilities of dissolving the boundaries between inside and out. The rear wall of Donovan Hill's villa extension can be opened up by means of a sliding louvred panel. This reveals a double-height dining zone that constitutes, in effect, an internal court, midway between outside and inside. In Brisbane's Hawthorne, Richard Kirk has created a spacious outdoor room by extending the living-dining area of his villa outwards as a double-height space roofed with a lightweight pergola. Such spatial fluidity is less suited to the cooler climate of Victoria, where architects generally have to content themselves with floor-to-ceiling glazing. The Toorak house designed by Andrew Norbury of Metier 3 has both its principal living area and master bedroom encased by full-height windows on three sides.

Though urban villas are generally set well back onto the site, their façades are often architecturally prominent, thereby preserving a sense of a street front. Upward-curving sheets of stainless steel distinguish the project by the architects Fender Katsalidis in Brighton, Melbourne: little wonder it has come to

Living area in Vaucluse designed by Ed Lippmann

Dining area in De Campo and Nevett's Toorak villa

Kitchen in the Brighton villa of Fender Katsalidis

Double wings of the Mosman villa of Alex Popov

be known as the Wave House. Similar curving metallic sheets are employed by Donaldson + Warn in their villa in Fremantle, Perth. The architects combine the metal with masonry walls and wooden panels to create a rich collage of materials, textures and colours. De Campo and Nevett develop a heavier, more monumental scheme for their Toorak villa. This is conceived as a showcase of insulated concrete technology, with alternating smooth and textured masonry surfaces relieved by timber balconies and overhangs. In the South Melbourne villa by the architects Swaney Draper, wooden louvres provide shade and privacy to the rear façade, while the front and sides preserve the original brick fabric of an old church.

Although urban villas are more generously scaled than their townhouse equivalents, in layout they are not all that different. Villas tend also to focus on a single living-dining space that occupies the main level, with kitchen bench and amenities to one side, as in Chris Clarke's economically planned, metallic house in Taringa, Brisbane. In larger projects such spaces are elongated and spatially articulated. The De Campo and Nevett villa has a linear succession of living, dining and kitchen areas, each stepping up from the other. They run from the front terrace with its swimming pool above the street to the back terrace beyond the kitchen. The double-height kitchen-dining area of the South Melbourne villa of Swaney Draper is roofed with a unique pointed vault that derives from the disused church, within which the new house was built. The lofty height of this zone affirms the primacy of cooking and eating in the life of this particular family. In contrast, the living area is only single height and can be closed off by sliding doors to achieve a more intimate atmosphere. Where space permits, living-dining areas may also be subdivided into formal and informal zones. Such is the case in the Brighton house of Fender Katsalidis, where living and dining activities for family and for guests focus on separate, though spatially linked, zones on different levels. A kitchen corridor with service facilities in Andrew Norbury's grandiosely planned Toorak residence separates the double-level formal living-dining area at the front from the single-level family area at the back. Laundry and storage facilities are located in between.

Vertical segregation of family life, with living and sleeping zones on different levels, is also possible in urban villas. In his tightly planned villa in Sydney's Vaucluse, Ed Lippmann raises the bedrooms over the living-dining area, but treats the whole of this upper level as a mezzanine balcony rather than a separate storey. Alex Popov, in his villa in Mosman, Sydney, splits the house into two distinct wings set at a slight angle to each other. One wing accommodates family living and dining at the upper level, with the children's bedrooms and playroom beneath; the other wing, defined by a gently curving wall, is devoted to the parents' needs. In Andrew Norbury's four-storey residence the children's bedrooms and entertainment area occupy an entire level of their own, with a private suite for the parents above.

Urban villas also offer unique possibilities for double family living, with a two-person apartment for an older couple combined with the principal family home. Michael Patroni's sprawling L-shaped villa in Peppermint Grove includes an apartment that is linked with the main house on two levels. Both residences open onto shaded decks that overlook the swimming pool. Another solution is that devised by Gary Marinko, who splits the apartment and principal residence of his Perth villa into two distinct zones situated at either end of a common court.

Gary Marinko's villa in Dalkeith

Formal living in the Toorak villa by Andrew Norbury of Metier 3

tropical tree house

left A path runs through the garden beside the small pool to the house

right Timber slatting characterizes the next door house, built by the same architects for the parents of one of the owners

Set in a small but lush garden in Brisbane's St Lucia, this house is dominated by a magnificent poinsettia tree. The husband and wife architectural team Peter Skinner and Elizabeth Watson Brown have devised a simple arrangement with the main living-kitchen area in the middle facing north towards the light and the tree. This is flanked on one side by an outdoor dining area partly projecting as a balcony, and on the other side by a master bedroom suite at a raised level, also with its own small balcony. A gallery running over the kitchen leads to a small den for the parents, while the children are accommodated in their own self-contained suite of rooms at a lower level. The repeated use of timber plywoods and decking and the large expanses of glass ensure that the interior harmonizes effortlessly with the tropical garden onto which it faces.

tropical tree house

above The living-kitchen area with outdoor dining at one end

opposite above The master bedroom overlooking the living area

right The twisted branches of
the poinsettia tree

reconstituted cottage

above The rebuilt timber cottage encasing the new residence

left A small planted side court lights the dining area

opposite left A spiral steel staircase ascends to the gallery linking the bedrooms

top The bedrooms are linked by a gallery that looks down on the living space

above The dining-kitchen area opens onto the garden

This family home by the architect Ed Lippmann in Sydney's Vaucluse partly occupies an old timber fisherman's cottage. This has been totally reconstituted as a tightly planned modernist residence with marine-grade plywood panels set in a simple steel structure. The ground level is a single space, the front of which serves as a living zone for the parents, with a dining-kitchen area for the whole family at the rear. The upper level with three bedrooms is conceived as a mezzanine with balcony-like side walls that do not touch the sloping ceiling, but nonetheless achieve the required privacy.

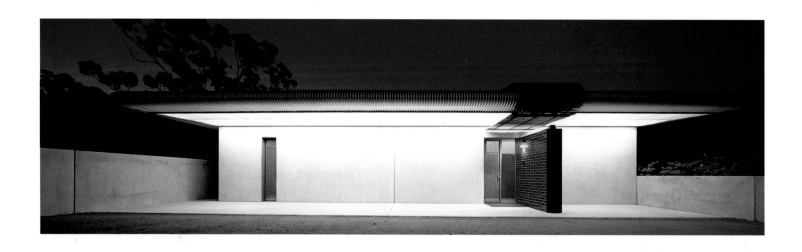

looking inwards

Turning its back on the street, this house designed by architect Gary Marinko in Perth's Dalkeith takes the form of an inward-looking residence entirely surrounded by walls. A perimeter passageway runs around three sides of the house, while internal light and ventilation are introduced by skylights and two courts, a smaller one for outdoor dining with a roof of metallic louvres, and a larger one open to the sky and planted, with a swimming pool beyond. The result is a series of spaces that flow seamlessly from indoors to outdoors. In addition to the usual living-dining zone, kitchen and master bedroom, the house also has a study and studio. At the end of the open court there is a self-contained apartment for the parents of one of the owners.

opposite above The street façade with its translucent fibreglass overhang reveals little about the interior of the house

opposite below The living-dining zone with sliding glass panels opening onto the larger open court

above Outdoor dining in the smaller court roofed by louvres and overlooked by the kitchen

looking inwards

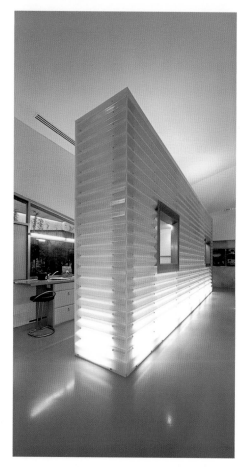

opposite above Bathroom with timber deck floor opening off the master bedroom

opposite below left Translucent screen wall separating the living zone from the kitchen

opposite below centre Skylit perimeter passageway

opposite below right The studio is sheltered by an internal diagonal canopy

right Kitchen looking out over the smaller roofed court

below Master bedroom with a wall of timber cupboards leading to the bathroom

outdoor room

This house for a family with three young children in Hawthorne responds to the sub-tropical climate of Brisbane by extending the enclosed living zone into an outdoor room defined by a delicately worked pergola. As conceived by the architect Richard Kirk, this outdoor room is roofed by a lightweight timber frame covered with corrugated translucent plastic sheeting that drops down on one side, ensuring both light

from above and privacy from next door. The double-height pergola is overlooked from one of the bedrooms and the connecting corridor at the upper level, while at the ground level it communicates with the living-dining-kitchen space. The simple timber construction of the pergola is echoed in the traditional timber frame of the house, expressed on the street façade by a grid of plywood panels.

opposite The double-height pergola at the end of the house encasing the outdoor living room

left A skylight illuminates the lime green walls of the staircase ascending to the bedrooms

above The dining-kitchen area with wooden and steel furniture on a dark grey concrete floor

below The master bedroom with pale polished woodwork and a bright pink wall; the side window has a glass panel that slides completely out of view

communicating with the garden

Extending outwards from a traditional terrace house in Sydney's Paddington, Andrew Nolan's sequence of two separate pavilions for living-dining and sleeping is dominated by an exquisitely crafted garden. Densely planted rooftop shrubs and bushes hang down over the windows of both pavilions. These are set at different levels, so that the courtyard garden overlooked by the living-dining pavilion is in fact the roof of the bedroom pavilion below. Both pavilions are sunk slightly beneath the level of the adjacent gardens and that of the lap pool which runs along one side of the house. The pale timber floors, seats and benches create a serene atmosphere, while the full-height sliding glass panels ensure maximum communication with the garden.

opposite above The living-dining pavilion with rooftop garden above and lap pool to one side

above The densely planted rooftop garden over the living-dining pavilion has a circular outdoor sitting area

opposite below The lap pool running from the old house beside the living-dining pavilion

below The sitting area in the living-dining pavilion is set at a slightly lower level than the surrounding garden

communicating with the garden

above The planted court between the old house and living-dining pavilion, with steps ascending to the rooftop garden and the lap pool to one side

right The kitchen is surrounded by glass and lit by a circular skylight; the lap pool beyond is set at bench height

left A pivoting glass panel links the old house with the garden

below The sitting area in the living-dining pavilion

climatically appropriate

Designed for a couple who own a contemporary art gallery, this comfortable villa in Fremantle, Perth, is a study in climatically appropriate materials and lighting. Here the architects Donaldson + Warn have created a composite construction, in which masonry and timber contrast with metallic sheets and glass. Thanks to innovative glazing, all the rooms on both levels of the house benefit from light flooding in from two sides, while open planning in the principal living-dining-kitchen area on the lower level enables cross ventilation. The somewhat severe geometry of the living spaces is animated by colourful art works.

above House from the street showing the bold juxtaposition of metallic sheets, plywood panels, masonry and glazing, all sheltered by generous overhangs

opposite below Entrance to the house, with colourful artwork by Daniel Argyle set at the base of a double-height timber-lined ventilation tower

above The northern, hotter side of the house, with walls of crushed limestone rock mixed with coloured sand and cement facing a planted garden

above Galvanized corrugated steel sheets line the southern, cooler side of the house, with its own smaller garden

dissolving boundaries

above The original house as seen from the street with the new double-height wing to the rear

In this project in New Farm, Brisbane, the architects Donovan Hill have extended a traditional Queensland house by adding a double-storey wing facing onto a walled garden with a long pool. The façade of the new wing contains a screen of metal louvres that slide to one side to reveal a double-height space for dining overlooked by a small internal balcony. The effect is to dissolve the distinction between inside and out. Metal and timber cladding and screens are used throughout the new wing, lending it a lightweight, transparent quality. These materials complement the spatial fluidity of the interior, which focuses on the double-height dining area. This is overlooked from within by a small balcony opening off the bedroom at the upper level.

above The new wing looks
out over a swimming pool that
continues the corridor axis of
the original house; the garage
to the left has a translucent
fibreglass wall that illuminates
the garden at night

left The sliding screen of
metal louvres in the closed
position

far left Double-height dining
area overlooked by a small
internal balcony

dissolving boundaries

above The kitchen with light flooding in from the ceiling, filtered through the skylight's bluish glass

right The kitchen-dining zone marks the transition from the original house to the new wing

below Rooftop dining around the skylight to the kitchen below

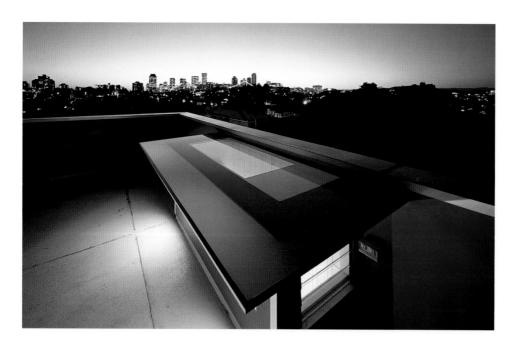

wave house

Built on a tight plot in Melbourne's Brighton, this imposing villa by the architects Fender Katsalidis is a showcase for a significant collection of Australian art. Elegantly sheathed in curving planes of stainless steel, the house surveys a walled garden with both an ornamental pond and swimming pool. The main level is a single open space divided into living area, kitchen-dining and formal dining, off which opens a small

TV den. An open staircase ascends to the bedrooms above. Below, tucked out of view, is a rumpus room and sunken court for the two teenage boys of the family and their friends. Steps from here lead up to the walled garden.

above The house from the garden showing the ornamental pond beside the wall lining the entrance path

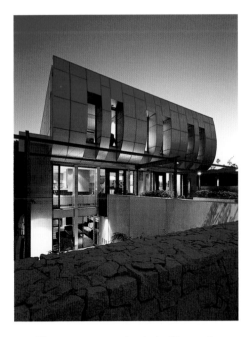

top The upper storey is clad with curving sheets of stainless steel containing deeply recessed windows; glass doors link the ground-floor living area and garden

above The children's sunken court, not visible from the street

above Small internal court at the upper level with sculpture by John Kelly

wave house

above Sliding corrugated glass door between the TV den and living area

right Skylight illuminating a painting by Mike Parr on the rear wall of the living area

opposite above Living area with fireplace separating it from the kitchen

opposite below Staircase with formal dining area beyond

spacious and tranquil

opposite above left The house from the street presents an unrelieved long limestone block

opposite above right The discreet entrance to the house at the end of a garden path

opposite below This end of the house is for more informal living; glass doors open onto a deck and pool

This spacious house for a family with three young sons in Toorak, Melbourne, designed by Andrew Norbury of Metier 3, demonstrates a meticulous control of luxurious materials, textures and colours. Warm tones prevail, mainly through the use of Mt Gambier limestone and Spanish and Italian marbles, and grey and beige fabrics in velvet and suede. The effect is a pervasive sense of tranquillity. The house has formal and informal living and dining on the ground level, with the children's bedrooms, guest bedroom and private cinema on the first upper level, and the master bedroom suite at the top, all linked by a staircase block and elevator.

top The kitchen is conceived as a service corridor linking the front and back of the house

above The lobby with staircase block has a view into the garden at the rear

spacious and tranquil

top Glass walls and a balcony surround the master bedroom at the top of the house

above The bathroom opening off the walk-through wardrobe

left The double-height living area at the front of the house is surrounded by windows on three sides; light is adjusted by electrically operated sunshades

metallic lightness

The architect Chris Clarke of Bligh Voller Nield previously worked with Norman Foster in the UK, which explains his commitment to steel-framed structures and metallic craftsmanship, as exemplified in this family home in Taringa in Brisbane. Rigorously modernist in approach, the house consists of a double-height, lightweight metallic frame built of low-cost standard components. Glass panels on two sides are interspersed with painted wall panels; the other two sides of the house, requiring greater privacy, have narrow window strips set into finely corrugated zincalum sheets. Similar

sheets, perforated for the sake of acoustics, are also occasionally used within the house to achieve a gleaming interior. The metallic structure is echoed in the steel furniture and fittings of the dining-kitchen zone, relieved by occasional splashes of bright colour.

below The double-height verandah wrapping around two sides of the house is slightly angled at the corner to create a teasingly false perspective

above The end wall of the double-height living-dining space is mostly of glass

above A large wall opening visually links the master bedroom to the dining-kitchen area below; it can be screened off by a sliding wooden panel

below Dining-kitchen area with floating bench and cabinets, and steel-framed dining table with acid-etched glass top

concrete minimalism

Smooth and textured concrete surfaces lend this house a solid, but severely minimalist appearance. Designed as a showpiece of insulated concrete technology by Christopher de Campo and Genevieve Nevett, the house is one of a pair of almost identical villas sharing a common party wall. The main level of the house, raised well above a leafy street in Melbourne's Toorak, is divided into outdoor terrace with pool, living area with steps leading up to the bedrooms, and dining zone and kitchen, each stepping up from the other towards the back of the house. Entry from the street is along a narrow pathway to one side.

above The house from the rear terrace, looking into the kitchen-dining zone, with the master bedroom above

above right The entry path running along the side of the house with its roughly textured concrete wall

right Front terrace with concrete tiles and swimming pool with cascade

concrete minimalism

above Metallic steps lead from the front
terrace and pool into the living area

far left Bathroom opening off the master bedroom at the top of the house

left Pre-cast concrete steps leading up to the bedrooms

below Living area with dining zone beyond

poolside drama

left The L-shaped wings of the family residence and two-person apartment flank the pool on two sides

below Dining area in the family residence with pivoting glass doors opening onto the pool

Architect Michael Patroni has conceived this villa in Peppermint Grove, Perth, as a dramatic series of interlocking planes, textures and colours. The whole composition is unified by a blade wall of heavy masonry that runs through the house, protruding boldly at either end. The villa accommodates a large family residence as well as a smaller two-person apartment.

Both are arranged on two levels in L-shaped formation around a swimming pool, from where the site dips down to a lily pond and tennis court. All the rooms face north, but are sheltered by generous overhangs. The audacious sun canopy that floats over the end of the blade wall creates a private outdoor sitting area for the apartment.

above Side entrance platform with different coloured wall panels

left Open staircase in the apartment

ecclesiastical domestic

Occupying the brick fabric of a disused and partly dismantled nineteenth-century church in South Melbourne, this house for a professional couple with young children is an inspired improvisation. The architects Swaney Draper have converted the nave into a double-height kitchen-dining area backed by a tall wooden panel. A gallery at the upper level hung with acoustic panels to counter the echo meets the challenge of accommodating a family within the lofty pointed vault of the original church. The apse of the church had already been dismantled, so the rear façade could be created anew. The glassed-in living area and master bedroom above are shielded from the western sun by wooden louvres.

above Paintings are displayed along the gallery linking the bedrooms at the upper level

left The transition from kitchen to dining to living areas is surmounted by the lofty pointed vault of the original church

opposite The rear façade projecting outwards from the original church nave, showing the living area with master bedroom and study den above

below Glazing with exterior louvres for privacy encases the bathroom that opens off the master bedroom

ecclesiastical domestic

left The living area with seating between large cherry-wood-framed lamps can be screened off from the kitchen-dining area by sliding doors

right The master bedroom with study den above

index of architects and designers

Allan Jack + Cottier
59 Buckingham Street, Surry Hills,
New South Wales 2010
tel (02) 9311 8222 fax (02) 9311 8200
email ajcarch@ajcarch.com.au
www.ajcarch.com.au
PROJECTS
Redfern, Sydney: Moore Park Gardens 26, 32

Tim Allison Associates
59 Buckingham Street, Surry Hills, New
South Wales 2010
tel (02) 9698 3133 fax (02) 9698 3722
email tim@taass.com.au
PROJECTS
Redfern, Sydney: Moore Parke Gardens,
penthouse 33–35

Ashton Raggatt McDougal
Level 11, 522 Flinders Lane, Melbourne 3000
tel (03) 9629 1222 fax (03) 9629 4220
email arm@a-r-m-com.au
www.a-r-m.com.au
PROJECTS
Canberra: National Museum of Australia 10

Michael Bialek
SJB Interiors, 25 Coventry Street, Southbank,
Victoria 3006
tel (03) 9686 2122 fax (03) 9686 2125
email interiors@sjb.com.au
www.sjb.com.au
PROJECTS
St Kilda Road, Melbourne: apartment 40–41

Bird de la Coeur Architects
35 Dundas Lane, Albert Park, Victoria 3206
tel (03) 9682 4566 fax (03) 9682 4577
email mail@bdlc.com.au
www.bdlc.com.au
PROJECTS
Albert Park, Melbourne: warehouse
conversion 124, 126
West Melbourne: warehouse conversion 127,
146–149

Nick Bochsler + Partners
5 Edward Street, Toorak, Victoria 3142

tel (03) 9827 2988 fax (03) 9827 2722
email bochsler@bochsler.com
www.bochsler.com
PROJECTS
South Yarra, Melbourne: apartment 18, 25,
27, 28–31

Gregory Burgess Architects
10 York Street, Richmond, Victoria 3121
tel (03) 9411 0600 fax (03) 9411 0699
email gba@gregoryburgessarchitects.com.au
www.gregoryburgess architects.com.au
PROJECTS
Melbourne, Sidney Myer Music Bowl 10, 12

Burley Katon Halliday
6A Liverpool Street, Paddington, New South
Wales 2021
tel (03) 9332 2233 fax (02) 9360 2048
email bkh@bkh.com.au
PROJECTS
East Sydney: Republic2, apartment 20–21, 26,
54–57

**Christopher de Campo and Genevieve
Nevett**
De Campo Architects, 116 Vale Street, East
Melbourne, Victoria 3022
tel (03) 9427 1177 fax (03) 9427 1217
email decampoarchitects@bigpond.com
PROJECTS
Toorak, Melbourne: urban villa 19, 158, 160,
194–197

Angelo Candalepas
Candalepas Associates, 64 Brenan Street,
Lilyfield, New South Wales 2040
tel (02) 9560 3188 fax (02) 9560 3199
email acarch@zip.com.au
PROJECTS
Paddington, Sydney: townhouse 110–111

Carr Design Group
Level 4, 31 Flinders Lane, Melbourne
3000
tel (03) 9654 8962 fax (03) 9650 5002
email melb@carrdesign.com.au
www.carrdesign.com.au

PROJECTS
St Kilda, Melbourne: Marquise apartments
52–53

Chris Clarke
Bligh Voller Nield Pty Ltd
365 St Pauls Terrace, Fortitude Valley,
Queensland 4006
tel (07) 3852 2525 fax (07) 3852 2544
email brisbane@bvn.com.au
www.blighvollernield.com.au
PROJECTS
Taringa, Brisbane: urban villa 19, 21, 160,
192–193

Codd Stenders Pty Ltd
163 Annerley Road, Dutton Park, Queensland
4102
tel (07) 3846 0877 fax (07) 3846 0977
email coddpart-second@powerup.com.au
PROJECTS
Fortitude Valley, Brisbane: townhouse 79,
92–95

Cunningham Martyn Design
18 Willis Street, Richmond, Victoria 3121
tel (03) 9428 2777 fax (03) 9428 2312
email office@cmdesign.com.au
PROJECTS
Fremantle, Perth: Western Australian
Maritime Museum 9, 12
Richmond, Melbourne: townhouse 86–87

Denton Corker Marshall
49 Exhibition Street, Melbourne, 3000
tel (03) 9654 4644 fax (03) 9654 7870
email melb@dentoncorkermarshall.com.au
www.dcm-group.com
PROJECTS
Melbourne: Melbourne Museum 9, 10
South Bank, Brisbane, arbour 10–11, 12

Donaldson + Warn Architects
36 Roe Street, Northbridge, Western
Australia 6003
tel (08) 9328 4475 fax (08) 9227 6558
email admin@donaldsonandwarn.com.au
www.donaldsonandwarn.com.au

tel (02) 92111220 fax (02) 9211 1554
www.lahznimmo.com
PROJECTS
Newtown, Sydney: townhouse extension
77–78, 96–97

Lippmann Associates
570 Crown Street, Surry Hills, New South
Wales 2010
tel (02) 9318 0844 fax (02) 9319 2230
www.lippmannassociates.com.au
PROJECTS
Vaucluse, Sydney: urban villa 21, 159, 161,
166–167

Gary Marinko Architects
M433, Faculty of Architecture, Landscape and
Visual Arts, The University of Western
Australia, 35 Stirling Highway, Crawley,
Western Australia 6009
tel (08) 9380 2797 fax (08) 9380 1082
email gary.marinko@uwa.edu.au
PROJECTS
Dalkeith, Perth: urban villa 19, 159, 161,
168–171

Marsh Cashman Architects
Studio 4, 113 Reservoir Street, Surry Hills,
New South Wales 2010
tel (02) 9211 4146 fax (02) 9211 4928
email mark@marshcashman.com.au
www.marshcashman.com
PROJECTS
Woollahra, Sydney: townhouse 79, 116–119

Sam Marshall
Architect Marshall, 53/61 Marlborough Street,
Surry Hills, New South Wales 2010
tel (02) 9310 7555 fax (02) 9310 4144
email sammarshall@ozemail.com.au
PROJECTS
Balmain, Sydney: townhouse extension 77,
98–99

**McBride Charles Ryan Architecture +
Interior Design**
Unit 4, 21 Wynnstay Road, Prahran, Victoria
3181
tel (03) 9510 1006 fax (03) 9510 0205
email mcrmail@bigpond.net.au
PROJECTS
Prahran, Melbourne: townhouses 76, 77,
104–107

**Alexander Michael – Interior Designer
and Architect**
52 Victoria Street, Potts Point, New South
Wales 2011
tel (02) 9360 4512 fax (02) 9360 3129
email siloboy@ozemail.com.au
www.siloboy.com
PROJECTS
Woolloomooloo, Sydney: apartment 21, 27,
64–67

Andrew Nolan Architect
1/48 Old Barrenjoey Road, Avalon Beach, New
South Wales 2107
tel (02) 9973 4355
email anarch@chilli.net.au
PROJECTS
Paddington, Sydney: urban villa 158, 174–177

Andrew Norbury
Metier 3, Level 3, Building 5,
658 Church Street, Richmond, Victoria 3121
tel (03) 9420 4000 fax (03) 9420 4001
email metier3@metier3.com.au
www.metier3.com.au
PROJECTS
Toorak, Melbourne: urban villa 159, 161,
188–191

O'Connor + Houle Architecture
70 Dow Street, South Melbourne, Victoria 3205
tel (03) 9686 7022 fax (03) 9686 7033
email beebee@ozonline.com.au
PROJECTS
South Yarra, Melbourne: townhouse 78,
100–101

Andrew Parr
SJB Interiors, 25 Coventry Street, Southbank,
Victoria 3006
tel (03) 9686 2122 fax (03) 9686 2125
email interiors@sjb.com.au
www.sjb.com.au
PROJECTS
Port Melbourne: HM@S Beach Apartments,
penthouse 21, 27, 60–61
St Kilda Road, Melbourne: apartment 40–41
St Kilda, Melbourne: townhouse 76–77, 80–81

Michael Patroni
Space Agency, 10 High Street, Fremantle,
Western Australian 6160
tel (08) 9430 5450 fax (08) 9430 9286

email patroni@spaceagency.com.au
PROJECTS
Peppermint Grove, Perth: urban villa 156–157,
158, 159, 161, 198–199

PTW Architects
Level 7, 9 Castlereagh Street
Sydney 2000
tel (02) 9232 5877 fax (02) 9221 4139
email info@ptw.com.au
www.ptw.com.au
PROJECTS
Sydney: East Circular Quay complex 42–47

Shelley Penn
4 Hoburd Drive, Woodend, Victoria 3442
tel (03) 5427 1294 fax (03) 5427 1994
email sjpenn@bigpond.com
PROJECTS
Richmond, Melbourne: warehouse conversion
21, 125, 138–139

Renzo Piano Building Workshop
Via Rubens 29, 16158, Genoa, Italy
tel (39) 0101 61711 fax (39) 0101 671350
www.rpwf.org
Represented in Australia by Innovarchi, Aurora
Place, 88 Phillip Street, Sydney 2000
tel (02) 9247 6191 fax (02) 9247 6148
email architects@innovarchi.com
www.innovarchi.com
PROJECTS
Sydney: Macquarie Apartments 25, 36–39

Alex Popov Architects
2 Glen Street, Milsons Point, New South
Wales 2061
tel (02) 9955 5604 fax (02) 9955 9258
email apa@alexpopov.com.au
PROJECTS
Mosman, Sydney: urban villa 160, 161

Allan Powell Pty Ltd
19 Victoria Street, St Kilda, Victoria 3182
tel (03) 9534 8367 fax (03) 9525 3615
email allan@allanpowell.com.au
PROJECTS
South Yarra, Melbourne: townhouse 78,
102–103

Harry Seidler & Associates
Level 5, 2 Glen Street, Milsons Point, New
South Wales 2061

tel (02) 9922 1388 fax (02) 9957 2947
email hsa@seidler.net.au
www.seidler.net.au
PROJECTS
Kings Cross, Sydney: Horizon Apartments 24

Six Degrees Architects
Top Floor, 100 Adderley Street, West
Melbourne, Victoria 3003
tel (03) 9321 6565 fax (03) 9328 4088
email 6deg@sixdegrees.com.au
www.sixdegrees.com.au
PROJECTS
Fitzroy, Melbourne: townhouse 79, 108–109

Stanic Harding Architects and Interiors Pty Ltd
123 Commonwealth Street, Surry Hills,
New South Wales 2010
tel (02) 9211 6710 fax (02) 9211 0366
email architects@stanicharding.com.au
www.stanicharding.com.au
PROJECTS
Surry Hills, Sydney: townhouse 78, 84–85

Swaney Draper Pty Ltd
376 Albert Street, East Melbourne,
Victoria 3002
tel (03) 9417 6162 fax (03) 3491 4480
email mail@swaneydraper.com.au
PROJECTS
South Melbourne: urban villa 160,
200–203

Kerstin Thompson Architects
169 Smith Street, Fitzroy, Victoria 3065
tel (03) 9419 4969 fax (03) 9419 4483
email kta@netspace.net.au
PROJECTS
Fitzroy, Melbourne: warehouse conversion
122–123, 124, 125, 126, 150–153

Tonkin Zulaikha Greer Pty Ltd
117 Reservoir Street, Surry Hills, New South
Wales 2010
tel (02) 9215 4900 fax (02) 9215 4901
email info@tzg.com.au
www.tzg.com.au
PROJECTS
Lilyfield, Sydney: townhouse 78
Potts Point, Sydney: apartment 25, 27,
50–51

Urban Design Architects
Level 9, 52 Collins Street, Melbourne 3000
tel (03) 9639 1666 fax (03) 9639 6566
email mtribe@urbandesign.com.au
www.urbandesign.com.au
PROJECTS
St Kilda, Melbourne: Marquise apartments 25,
27, 52–53

Elizabeth Watson Brown Architects
88 Gailey Road, St Lucia, Queensland 4067
tel (07) 3870 7760 fax (07) 3870 4752
email ewb@eis.net.au
www.ewbarchitects.cjb.net
PROJECTS
St Lucia, Brisbane: urban villa 158, 162–165

Willemsen Development Corporation
40 Riverview Parade, Surfers Paradise,
Queensland 4217
tel (07) 5526 7504 fax (07) 5526 7509
email design@willemsengroup.com
www.willemsengroup.com
PROJECTS
Surfers Paradise, Queensland: Sentinel
apartments 18, 24–25

Wood Marsh Pty Ltd
466 William Street, West Melbourne, Victoria
3003
tel (03) 9329 4920 fax (03) 9329 4977
email wm@woodmarsh.com.au
www.woodmarsh.com.au
PROJECTS
Melbourne: Australian Centre for
Contemporary Art 8–9, 10,
Prahran, Melbourne: warehouse conversion
18, 20, 126, 127, 132–135

index of locations

acknowledgments

Both photographer and author are indebted to all the architects who have provided information and assistance, as well as to the many home owners who tolerated the unwelcome intrusion of investigative visits and photographic shoots at different times of day and night. Among the colleagues and friends who have been generous with their advice and time are Brit Andreson, Haigh Beck, Joan Bowers, Brett Bush, Jackie Cooper, Beverley Garlick, Anna Horne, Davina Jackson, Colin James, Alexander Michael, Anna Mow, Neville Quarry, Graham Sands, Zdenka Underwood, Deborah White and Sabrina Snow. George Michell also benefited from discussions with John Fritz.

Before and during site visits, John Gollings relied on the unstinting support and production efforts of his assistant/producer Emma Cross, often through long and arduous sessions. At the Gollings photographic studio, Kirstin Gollings assisted by Sian Hinschen prepared all of the digital material for the publishers with extraordinary diligence and expertise. Sue Shanahan supervised the overall progress of the project and collated all the material with her customary proficiency and patience, without which this project could never have been completed.

John Gollings is grateful to James Eiffe, Brett Boardman, Peter Clarke and Carl Linstrom for permitting one each of their photographs to be included in this volume (pages 79, 96, 107 and 160 respectively).

Constant encouragement was offered by Peter Shaw at the Melbourne office of Thames & Hudson.

John Gollings and George Michell